PHILOSOPHY FOR
POLAR EXPLORERS

Also by Erling Kagge

Silence: In the Age of Noise

Walking: One Step at a Time

PHILOSOPHY FOR
POLAR EXPLORERS

Erling Kagge

Translated from the Norwegian by
KENNETH STEVEN

Pantheon Books, New York

Grateful acknowledgement is made to Kenneth Steven for his translation of the text and to Diane Oatley for her translation of the foreword.

Library of Congress Cataloging-in-Publication Data
Name: Kagge, Erling, author.
Title: Philosophy for Polar explorers / Erling Kagge ;
translated from the Norwegian by Kenneth Steven.
Other titles: *Alt jeg ikke lærte på skolen*. English.
Description: First American edition. New York : Pantheon Books, 2020.
Translation of author's *Alt jeg ikke lærte på skolen*, published in 2005.
Includes bibliographical references.
Identifiers: LCCN 2020019534 (print). LCCN 2020019535 (ebook).
ISBN 9781524749118 (hardcover). ISBN 9781524749125 (ebook).
Subjects: LCSH: Kagge, Erling—Travel—Polar regions. Kagge, Erling—
Philosophy. Polar regions—Discovery and exploration—Norwegian.
Explorers—Conduct of life.
Classification: LCC G875.K34 A3 2020 (print) |
LCC G875.K34 (ebook) | DDC 910/.01— dc23
LC record available at lccn.loc.gov/2020019534
LC ebook record available at lccn.loc.gov/2020019535

www.pantheonbooks.com

Jacket photograph by Arctic-Images/Stone/Getty Images
Jacket design by Kelly Blair

Printed in the United States of America
First American Edition
1 3 5 7 9 8 6 4 2

For Ingrid, Solveig, and Nor

Snow Globe, Ceal Floyer

Contents

Foreword:
Grounding Myself in Nature

When I am feeling cold beneath the open sky, there's an easy way to warm up: I pull the hood of my anorak over my head, draw the zipper up to my throat, and pick up my pace. When my body heats up, first in my torso and then down my arms to my wrists, and finally underneath my fingernails, I can stop. Then I take out a mandarin, peel it, and slowly suck out the juice by pressing each section gently against the roof of my mouth with my tongue.

Suddenly I feel connected: connected with the person who planted the tree, with the water the tree has drunk through its roots, the earth that cushions these roots, the branch that has carried the mandarin from fertilization to fruition, and the sun that has helped to ripen it. And I feel grateful: grateful for being warm again and for the feeling of being in contact with the rhythms of nature.

At other times when I'm out on a walk, it's as if I'm not thinking at all. I seldom notice any activity along the way. My mind goes into hibernation, and only very occasionally a solitary thought will cross it: how the snowflakes beneath my skis are created by a tiny drop of water, ten or twenty kilometres above the Earth's surface, becoming, piece by piece, a six-sided prism, consisting of 90 per cent air. How it then floats down through the atmosphere and lands on the ground in front of me. No two snowflakes are alike, and none follow the same route. They are often, though not always, symmetrical. Until my skis compress them, that is.

Nature has its own language, experiences, and consciousness. It tells us where we come from and what we should do on the road ahead. I grew up without a television or a car (my father considered both to be dangerously unhealthy) and spent a lot of my free time in the forest, by the sea, and in the mountains, so I have been spoon-fed this knowledge. Today, when the modern world expects us to be available at all times, grounding yourself in nature can be hard. I forget about it sometimes, and when I look around, I get the feeling that many people forget about it all the time.

Nature is about diversity. The more I remove myself from nature and the more I increase my availability to the modern world, the more restless I become. The more unhappy too. I am no scientist, but my experience has been that, to a large extent, feelings of insecurity, loneliness, and depression stem from the flattening of the world that occurs when we are alienated from nature. There is, of course, much to be said in favour of man-made environments and new technology, but our eyes, nose, ears, tongue, skin, brain, hands, and feet were not created for choosing the road of least resistance. Mother Earth is 4.54 billion years old, so it seems arrogant to me when we don't listen to nature and instead blindly place our trust in human invention.

In 2010, my Norwegian friend Børge Ousland, the Icelandic polar explorer Haraldur Örn Ólafsson, and I crossed Vatnajökull, Iceland's largest glacier. We travelled light and carried all the food and equipment we needed on our respective small runnerless sleds, called pulks. By volume, Vatnajökull is the largest glacier in Europe. It is made up of 3,100 cubic kilometres of ice and covers 8,100 square kilometres of south-east Iceland. As is often the case with Icelandic glaciers, there are a number of volcanoes beneath the ice. While we were on our way across it, a volcanic eruption broke out in the neighbouring glacier, Eyjafjallajökull. Hundreds of people were immediately evacuated and the air traffic above a large part of Europe was suspended because of the clouds of volcanic ash. We were never in danger, but the experience showed me how a small volcano erupting in a remote region of Iceland can have huge consequences for an entire continent. Large volcanic eruptions can change the whole world. I sometimes wonder if we need natural disasters like these to remind us of the Earth's rhythms and forces. I'd like to think that's not the case, and that people can choose to reconnect with nature from time to time in a more peaceful way.

During the first twelve years of my life, my parents sent me outdoors in all kinds of weather. I believe that

at first I liked it, but then I grew bored with it in my
early teens. I began putting my energy into indoor
activities and partying instead. Seven or eight years
later, I started yearning for nature again. I missed the
forest, the mountains, and the ocean, the feeling of
physical exertion in the outdoors. It was a yearning
that came from inside me, a deep-felt need for close
contact with elements not made by machines. To feel
the sun, rain, cold, wind, mud, and water on my body.
To listen.

I can identify with some of the thoughts Ernest Shackleton described towards the end of his life as an explorer: "We had seen God in his splendours, heard the text that Nature renders. We had reached the naked soul of man."

I have begun to wonder more about the paths I have chosen, and those I have taken less consciously, to arrive at my current location. In thinking about this, I found myself confronted with a series of questions: Why push your endurance to the breaking point? And why, with frostbite, blisters, and hunger still fresh in your mind, would you choose to do it all again? When I started doing expeditions, I was most interested in everything hidden behind the horizon and not what was right in front of me. If I went out walking, I wanted to walk for a long time and cover great distances. I had not yet discovered the pleasure of a short walk. Later, with teenage daughters, a demanding job, and a newfound interest in art, I became aware that my life had gradually changed, and I directed my thoughts inwards. This resulted in two books—*Silence: In the Age of Noise* and *Walking: One*

Step at a Time—both of which are, in different ways, about the silence we carry inside us.

Most important for me, all three books—this book and the other two—are about being in contact with nature. One of the things I have learned as an explorer is that every so often along the journey, you have to stop and recalibrate, to take stock of unexpected events or changes in the weather. This book is a recalibration of sorts.

PHILOSOPHY FOR
POLAR EXPLORERS

1.

Setting My Own Compass

As a child, if I could dream it or imagine it, then I could do it too. Everything that can be dreamed up between two ears is possible when one doesn't know any better. I could do everything I wanted: become a World Cup football player, sail around the globe, ski across the great wastelands, climb mountains, live like Muhammad Ali, kiss the prettiest girl in the class, save the world from destruction, grow up to be like Albert Schweitzer, be a fireman, escape from Alcatraz, travel to the moon or to Mars.

I started school late and was among the bottom three in the class academically for twelve consecutive years, I wasn't particularly good at sports, and my circle of friends was small. I really didn't seem to have anything going for me. I never did anything extraordinary as a child. But I dreamed about it. And I never stopped dreaming.

At some point it dawned on me that my chances of being a fireman, a footballer, an astronaut, and a superhero all at once were limited. My dreams became more focused.

In 1990, Børge and I became the first to reach the North Pole without the assistance of snowmobiles, dogs, or depots. In 1993, I became the first to walk alone to the South Pole—unlike most solo expeditioners, I chose to have no contact with the outside world. Then, in 1994, I climbed Mount Everest. In doing all of this, I fulfilled my ambition to become the first to reach the Earth's three poles on foot.

This is, in part, an account of the dreams and ideas that never lost their hold on me and that led to these adventures. These dreams evolved and, in time, were brought to fruition by curiosity and personal ambition. It's interesting to note that while on these journeys to my original goals, I began to set new ones . . . to see fresh horizons and more exciting possibilities. I find it difficult to imagine this world without believing that there is still more to be done and experienced.

"I'd have done anything to experience what you did," someone said to me after I made my first voyage across the Atlantic. I was twenty; we had just reached Barbados from Cape Verde off West Africa, and I had swum to land from the boat and just put my feet on terra firma for the first time in a long two weeks. Over the years many others have said the same thing to me. But I am not certain they really did want those experiences. If they did, they might have tried.

When I was a kid, I was a great admirer of the Norwegian explorer Thor Heyerdahl. One of the first books I read was about his voyage in 1947 on the raft *Kon-Tiki* from Callao in Peru to the Tuamotu Islands in Polynesia. Heyerdahl had a fear of water after having twice almost drowned as a child; nonetheless, he had a dream of crossing the Pacific on this handmade raft of balsa logs. Six people sailed with the *Kon-Tiki*—which was a facsimile of the prehistoric rafts the native people of Peru had built—westwards for 101 days across the Pacific in order to prove that people could've settled Polynesia in this way.

I was hugely pleased and a little surprised when, in the autumn of 1994, I was invited to Heyerdahl's eightieth-birthday celebrations, and I looked forward to having the opportunity to pay my respects. At the party lots of Heyerdahl's old friends gave speeches. They all praised—as was fitting—this man who'd discovered so much, the *Kon-Tiki* man. Several of them also talked about the opportunities they'd had to travel with Heyerdahl, although for one reason or another—studies, partner, family, work—they'd been prevented from doing so. The speeches were long. Throughout them I watched Heyerdahl, who smiled to himself as he listened, and I came to a realization. "The crucial difference between everyone else and you, Mr. Heyerdahl," I said to myself, "is that you made your own choices and didn't let others make them for you. When you had opportunities, you took them and thought about all the obstacles later."

Had the speakers just chosen what seemed the

safest option? Had they allowed others to make
the decision for them? Or perhaps they considered
their obligations at home weightier? The difference
between Heyerdahl and the others seemed to be that
Heyerdahl was following his own dream, while they
were trying to follow the dreams of someone else.

Buridan's Donkey is the first philosophical puzzle I remember reading. It is about a donkey standing between two identical haystacks and illustrates what happens when one refuses to make a choice. The distance to each of the haystacks is exactly the same, and it's impossible for the donkey to decide which haystack to walk to and consume first. Time passes, the donkey weighs up the choice, never comes to a decision, and in the end dies of hunger midway between the two haystacks.

The South Pole, perhaps? Alone, then, to the South Pole! For me the decision was made the moment the idea came to mind. Thereafter all I had to do was think through how it might be achieved in rational detail. Had I turned things on their head—done the fine-tuning first, then nailed the idea, then thought it through to see if it was workable before deciding whether or not I'd pursue it—I'd never have made it.

For me there's a great joy in setting targets. My own North Poles. Not Heyerdahl's, not my neighbour's, not my family's. I'll do it! I'll sail across the Atlantic, help someone in need, buy a bottle of champagne, say no to a temptation, write a book like this, start a publishing house, become a lawyer, start a family. In times to come, what we may regret are the chances we didn't take, the initiative we didn't show. What we didn't do. If you say it's impossible and I say it's possible, we're probably both right.

Sometimes I wonder what has become of all the dreams and ambitions that I never did anything with. I wonder where they are. I don't think I'd have to look very hard to find them. As many have noted before me, it's easier to take ourselves out of our dreams than to take our dreams out of us.

2.

Getting Up Early

Getting up at the right time in the morning is a polar explorer's greatest challenge. That's as true today as it was in the age of Ernest Shackleton, Roald Amundsen, and Fridtjof Nansen. So when I'm asked what the hardest thing is out there on the ice, I'm never in any doubt as to my answer. There's something unspeakably tempting about remaining in one's sleeping bag when it's down to minus fifty-four degrees Celsius, as it was at times on our way to the North Pole. It beats crawling out of that sleeping bag and feeling as though you have been frozen up to your chin in ice, like a sinner in the Ninth Circle of Dante's Inferno. To save on weight, Børge and I had neither sufficient fuel to heat the tent—only 0.2 litre white gas per person per day—nor extra underwear, so for the sixty-three days and nights the expedition lasted I didn't undress once.

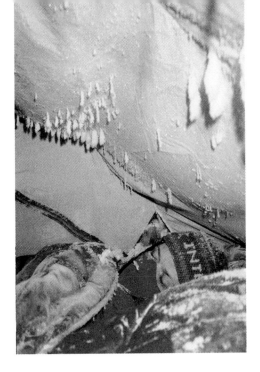

"This is the roughest thing I've done since I was born," Børge wrote in his diary. On that journey there was no shortage of reasons to remain in a sleeping bag: frostbite, illness, tiredness, and injury. At low points we told each other that in the grand scheme of things this was a relatively short period of our lives, and that before long we'd be able to rest.

It was no different on the journey to the South Pole.

In those situations the thought of getting up is far worse than the act itself. It's like an Alfred Hitchcock film: there's no terror in the bang itself, only in the anticipation of it. Because the greatest danger is— as in a good horror film—putting things off. Get up I must. It's simply a question of whether I put it off for five minutes or five hours.

It took many years before I stopped being surprised that it was seldom as cold outside as it sounded when I was lying in my sleeping bag listening to the wind in the rigging or tugging at the flysheet of the tent. Roald Amundsen, the first man to reach the South Pole, wrote in his account that it was on the days when the grounds for staying in the sleeping bag were most persuasive that things went best—once they got going. On expeditions, as in life generally, the final step is dependent on the first.

As an office worker, it has struck me that the greatest challenge remains the same. It's about getting up at the right time, regardless of where I may be and what I did the evening before. So over time I've evolved from a late sleeper to an early riser as the demands on me have increased. This might not work for everyone, but it definitely works for me.

What I know of discipline I learned above the tree line. If it's cold, it's tempting to stop walking earlier than planned, and if you're very hungry, it's all too easy to nibble at a bit of tomorrow's ration. At home it's perhaps not so earth-shattering if I stay in bed or put off making an unpleasant telephone call. But out there I suffered immediate consequences when I procrastinated. For these reasons, I'm in no doubt that my experiences in the great outdoors have made me far more disciplined at home. Besides, the day is made so much better once the unpleasant things have been dispensed with.

3.

Training Myself in Optimism

A classic Zen Buddhist pilgrim's tale concerns the wrestler O-nami, meaning "Great Waves." O-nami was hugely strong and really understood the art of wrestling. When he was practising, he even got the better of his own teacher, but when spectators were present, he became so shy that his own pupils could put him on the mat. O-nami decided he would visit a Zen master and ask for help. Hakuju, a wandering teacher, had taken up residence in a small temple close by, so O-nami sought him out and explained his difficulties. "Great Waves is your name," said the teacher, "so stay here in the temple tonight. Imagine you are waves. No longer are you a fearful wrestler. You are the waves themselves that sweep away all in their path, consume everything in their way. Do this, and you will be the greatest wrestler in the land." The teacher withdrew. O-nami sat deep in thought and tried to imagine himself as waves. As the night sped by, the waves grew greater and greater. They swept the flowers from the vases. Even Buddha in his sanctuary was overwhelmed. Before the break of day that entire temple had become the ebb and flow of a veritable ocean. In the morning the teacher came and saw O-nami sitting and meditating, the ghost of a smile on his lips. He patted the wrestler's shoulder. "Nothing can disturb you now," he said. "You are waves. You will sweep away everything before you." That very day, O-nami joined the wrestling bouts and won. Thereafter no one in Japan could defeat him.

"The struggle lies between the ears, not in the feet," I wrote after the journey to the North Pole. If the body's able but we can't convince the head, we won't get anywhere.

I remember asking my daughter Nor, who was eight at the time, if she still believed she could achieve anything she wanted in life. "Yes, but I think Solveig"—her younger sister, who was five—"believes it even more than me," she answered. I didn't quite know how to persuade Nor that nothing had

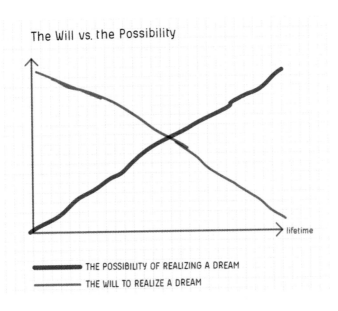

The Will vs. the Possibility

lifetime

THE POSSIBILITY OF REALIZING A DREAM
THE WILL TO REALIZE A DREAM

changed . . . and that naysayers were best ignored for the time being. Later in life, Nor will realize that she can't do everything she wants, but I think it is better if that realization does not occur too early in life.

Naïve optimism is something children seem to possess innately. In a child's mind the world is changing, we are changing; the whole world remains unexplored. I believe they are right. There is no finish line. The most beautiful sea hasn't been crossed yet.

The best advice I ever got was from an elephant trainer in the jungle outside Bangalore. I was doing a hike through the jungle as a tourist. I saw these large elephants tethered to a small stake. I asked him: "How can you keep such a large elephant tied to such a small stake?" He said: "When the elephants are small, they try to pull out the stake and they fail. When they grow large, they never try to pull out the stake again." —Vivek Paul, adjunct professor, Stanford University

---

Put simply, optimism is the belief that the conditions of things can and will get better. But being optimistic obviously shouldn't mean being careless. The American psychologist Martin Seligman advocates what he calls "flexible optimism," which factors in risks rather than blind belief in positive outcomes. When the cost of miscalculating is severe, then it is time to be decidedly pessimistic. But when there's little to lose by being gung-ho and optimistic, then go for it!

If you are close to sinking in the middle of the northern Atlantic, as my friends Hauk Wahl and Arne Saugstad and I were, sailing back from the Caribbean in the winter of 1984, then telling yourself that there's no way to stop the water pouring into your boat is probably not going to help: you'll just give up. At the office I'm quite happy to listen to and consider objections, but I seldom dwell on them unnecessarily. If there's something concrete that can be done to change the situation, then that's all well and good. I may still feel sad and depressed as a result of criticism, but I let it go more easily today than in the past. I really do believe that it pays to try to have a positive attitude and, mental bat in hand, to try to whack away as much of the negativity as possible. If it doesn't disappear the first time around, then you can always try again.

One of my first childhood heroes was the Englishman

Daley Thompson, who was the world's best decathlete for ten years. He believed defeats were temporary setbacks: "I'm good at it until proved otherwise." Thompson usually trained three times a day because he reckoned the other competitors would be content to train twice, and that would put him ahead of the field. On Christmas Day he was careful to train twice, in the event that one of the others would train that day too. "If I trained twice, I would still know that I was up on them." But it wasn't just his body he was training. He was also cultivating a mindset of self-belief informed by his physical exercise. According to Thompson, he was competing first and foremost against himself, but as he always trained harder than his competitors, he knew in his own mind he was better prepared. And his competitors knew it too, which made them pessimistic. In the seventies and eighties, when battles between Thompson and his competitors raged, it seemed almost predetermined that Thompson would win—if only by nothing more than a few hundredths of a second. And he did.

I am reminded of the Zen story of the great warrior

Nobunaga, which emphasizes the importance of optimism. Nobunaga attacked an enemy force which outnumbered him ten to one. His odds weren't looking good. But Nobunaga turned to the spiritual world for help. He stopped at a Shinto sanctuary and told the troops that, after praying, "I will toss a coin. If heads come up, we will win; if tails, we will lose. Destiny holds us in her hand." He prayed silently, then tossed the coin. It came up heads, and his soldiers, inspired by the omen, crushed the enemy. "No one can change the hand of destiny," remarked his attendant sagaciously after the battle was won. "Indeed not," said Nobunaga, showing him the coin he had tossed. It was double-headed.

4.

Learning Not to Fear Greatness

When I was fifteen I cycled from my home in Oslo to
Strömstad in Sweden to visit a girl I was in love with.
It's a journey of about ninety miles and it took me
half the day. I was standing outside her house—I still
remember the address: Tallstigen 4—stretching,
when it suddenly hit me that I might just as well go
home. Not bother to ring the doorbell. I was surprised
at my own reaction. She was no less gorgeous than
when I'd decided to cycle to visit her, but now
that I was finally within sight of my objective, I
completely lost the desire to go any farther. And
it wasn't because I felt the road itself had been the
most significant element, but because I simply didn't
dare to experience the next chapter. Since then I've
encountered similar tendencies in people I have
met: people who have been on the verge of attaining
something, only to pull back. A friend finally got the

job and salary he'd been striving for, along with great opportunities for progression within the company. But instead of going the full distance, he found he didn't give a damn; he couldn't or wouldn't go on.

In the Italian film *Cinema Paradiso,* from 1988, an elderly man by the name of Alfredo tells the story of a soldier who was in love with a princess. He realized that a man of his standing had no chance with her at all, but he still wouldn't give up. One day the princess told him that if he stood outside her window for a hundred days and nights she would marry him. The soldier took up position outside her house. The days and weeks passed. He endured rain, wind, snow, and cold. On the ninetieth day he could barely stand up straight, tears flowed down his cheeks, but he wouldn't give up. On the ninety-ninth day, when he had all but won his beloved, he gave up. Without further ado, he just left. I saw that film with a friend. She reckoned he'd given up because in the future he wouldn't be able to cope with the humiliation of what the princess had put him through. A psychiatrist friend thought the soldier had walked away because he finally knew his goal was within reach, and there was no challenge anymore. Either could be right, but I can't help thinking that he left his place after almost 2,400 hours because he did not dare to remain in love—the greatest of all feelings—when the princess was no longer a distant dream. He was abandoning a future that was uncertain in preference for something predictable. This business of "winning the princess and half the kingdom"—as the Norwegian folk tales put it—needn't necessarily be the start of a wonderful story. It's not automatically the case that one lives happily ever after. Perhaps that's when the real problems begin, and the reason the fairy tales end where they do.

I've travelled to a hundred countries and have met thousands of people, and I'm in no doubt that the majority of us undervalue ourselves. It seems that many of us are afraid of our own greatness, and so we make ourselves less than we are. It's not always a fear we express—it could be an idea lurking in the background, putting a damper on things.

Almost like a little voice inside each and every one of us saying that it's time to give up, that it's not worth continuing, that we've come far enough. It's easy to reject the exciting in favour of the safe, and forget that we have numerous opportunities for new positive experiences.

I don't mean that it's suddenly up to you and me to believe in our own greatness at the expense of self-reflection or realism. And by greatness, I don't mean superiority. Greatness is relative. An acquaintance of mine is afraid of opening bills that arrive in the mail. For him it would be an achievement to adapt to the world, to take control of things and avoid bankruptcy. Opening envelopes isn't normally about strength, but for him it is. What I have in mind when I talk about greatness is the potential of each and every individual to overcome obstacles. Small ones and, at times, great ones.

It is easy to fear greatness because the more you try to achieve, the more likely you are to put yourself in a situation in which you risk failure. The fear of looking like an idiot if we fail is perhaps what makes us sweep our dreams under the rug. It often feels safer not to try than to try and not succeed. I still remember sitting in the sauna after a skiing trip with a friend barely a year before Børge, Geir Randby (who had come up with the idea for the whole expedition, but who unfortunately was injured early on and had to pull out), and I were due to leave for the North Pole. I asked him what he thought the public response would be if we were to fail. What would it mean for me? "Don't give a damn about it!" was his immediate response. At the time I thought he was being a bit dismissive of what were, in my opinion, justifiable concerns. Later, once I'd thought it through, I began to see that with such worries I might as well plonk myself down on the sofa with the remote instead of going to the North Pole.

Standing out from the crowd can be tantamount to being lonely. Research in the United States has shown that a common reason for the collapse of a friendship circle is the greater professional success of one party, who then stands out from the rest in an unwelcome way. Generally it's the people who don't do as well who decide to cool the friendship or end it completely. We can find the same conclusion in the title of one of Morrissey's songs: "We Hate It When Our Friends Become Successful." We feel like it should have been us.

Sometimes I forget that there are other opportunities out there that don't cross my path every day. For two years at the beginning of the 1990s I was a solicitor at Norsk Hydro, a leading Norwegian energy company. Immediately after starting I began to feel that the firm, or at least a large part of it, was dependent on me—that my activities were essential. A positive attitude certainly, but utterly crazy. To believe your work is terribly important is, according to the British philosopher Bertrand Russell, "one of the symptoms of an approaching nervous breakdown." At the same time I often felt dependent on my employer. Along with many of my colleagues, I imagined my workplace to be central to my world. I was deceiving myself and forgetting that I could choose another path. What is promised in a high-powered career in corporate law is, of course, more corporate law. Eventually I left to walk to the South Pole. My employer did better than ever the following year.

One of the major advantages of not fearing our own greatness is that we will cease to fear it in others. "I could have done that too" is something I've thought many times when I've heard what others have done. Maybe, but I didn't. If I start bitterly thinking about all the reasons why that person isn't any better than me and shouldn't have achieved what I didn't, then all I do is let the small-minded side of myself get the better of me. Either I should have done whatever it was or else I should simply think about it differently. Had I been smarter, I'd have been happy for the person and thereby felt good myself, instead of embarrassed. Keeping small-mindedness at bay is an art, and the surest way to achieve it is by giving ourselves room to achieve and accepting that the achievements of others don't take away from that space.

I have a suspicion about where at least some of these feelings that conspire to diminish us come from: most boys and men I know have a father complex. I do. My father had a father complex, as did my grandfather and probably my great-grandfather. I believe many of our reactions to situations in our adult lives can be explained by the relationship—or lack thereof—between father and son. This complex is a central theme in everything from the Old Testament and the return of the Prodigal Son to *The Lion King,* a movie I have seen twenty or thirty times with my children. We are in timeless company.

I love my father deeply, despite remembering how he has expressed his doubts about my abilities before and after every adventure since I was a teenager. Other people could be negative too, but there's something about the terse comments—"You will never make it" or "It's impossible"—when they're made by a father. They cut deeper. But even more than that, I can remember how I wanted to please him. The first time I succeeded in doing that was when I returned from the South Pole. His accolades were more satisfying than any other. With my mother, it was different. She loved me no matter what I did.

As I've grown older, I've come to realize that my

father, like most other fathers, probably didn't mean much harm by his criticisms or rebukes. My parents had good reasons for being worried, as I wasn't always the easiest of sons. Today I am more of a can-do father to my three daughters than a can't-do one—but it is not easy to find a good balance. Even pretty innocent negative comments can leave a mark. If you're told as a child that you can't draw, it's easy to believe it to be true for the rest of your life.

5.
Not Mistaking
Probability for Possibility

"We have to differentiate between what is completely impossible and what is merely improbable," writes the Norwegian philosopher and mountaineer Arne Næss. Nothing is completely impossible, he insists—just less and less probable. All eventualities while you are alive exist on a kind of "possibility meter" which goes from 0.1 to 99.9 per cent certainty.

On expeditions as well as in daily life, I find Næss's logic very helpful. When I consider the history of polar exploration, it is full of stories of people who survived against all the odds. On the night of October 15, 1872, for example, the American ship *Polaris* was hit by an iceberg off the north-west coast of Greenland. Nineteen of the survivors—including five children—ended up stranded on an iceberg. They landed in one of the harshest, most windswept corners of the globe without adequate equipment or sufficient sustenance. For six months they drifted on the iceberg through the very coldest season of the Arctic year. All told, they travelled some 3,000 kilometres south, from Smith Sound down past Baffin Island and the entrance to Hudson Bay, eventually ending up off the coast of Newfoundland on April 30, 1873. I have travelled in the region myself, well equipped, and for me it's still difficult to comprehend that anyone could survive for that many weeks on an iceberg with such minimal provisions. Of course, they came close to drowning, freezing to death, and starving; but they built igloos and shelters for themselves from ice and snow, and hunted seals. When they were eventually rescued by a whaling crew, one of the sailors asked if they'd actually spent the night on the iceberg. One of the survivors described bursting out laughing for the first time in months. People's immediate reaction was one of incredulity, both that such a well-fitted ship as *Polaris* could be wrecked in the first place, and that it was possible that anyone could survive for half a year on an iceberg without being prepared for the ordeal in the least.

When Geir, Børge, and I decided to walk to the North Pole, few believed we stood a chance. Perhaps it even seemed impossible to us at the beginning, but from then on the probability that we would manage it began to rise in line with our preparations.

Before I travelled to the South Pole alone, there were some who thought I was a touch mad, while others reckoned I would go mad on the journey. At school my teachers thought that because of my dyslexia and lack of concentration, writing a book would be impossible for me. As would, for that matter, having anything to do with a publishing house.

What is humanly possible changes, and we live in a time when most things are changing faster than ever before. Since the dawn of time, human beings have viewed the wings of birds and dreamed of flying. It was impossible until the right materials and developments in physics presented themselves more than a hundred years ago. According to the Royal Geographical Society, and to most others with an opinion on the subject, drifting right across the Arctic was an impossibility until Fridtjof Nansen and his men did so in the mid-1890s. Until recently it was considered impossible for a human to travel to Mars, but now it's only a matter of time before someone sets out on what will be a journey of about 140 million miles (the exact distance varies).

The American cult documentary film *Dogtown and Z-Boys* recounts the history of the skateboarding fraternity in California in the 1970s, a small group of pioneers who subsequently turned the sport upside down by experimenting with what was possible with a skateboard. As Tony Alva, one of the film's subjects, says at one point, they could envisage the moves they wanted to do; they just didn't know if it was possible to actually do them. The problem was that there was nowhere suitable for them to try out what they had choreographed. Then serendipity struck. In the course of one summer, everything changed in a way that no one could have imagined. A great drought hit

California and all the swimming pools quickly became bone-dry. Without asking the owners' permission, the gang from Dogtown laboriously set to work cleaning out these unused pools. With their solid surfaces and their sharp curves, they were perfect for skateboarding. So it was that Tony Alva, Jay Adams, and their companions were finally able to put their ideas into practice, and thereby build the foundations of a global skateboard culture. What had been barely possible for a cluster of individuals to realize, all at once became something the masses could attempt.

There was a time when it was quite inconceivable that ordinary citizens could effect dramatic change by writing letters to heads of state and generals across the globe. Then, one day, the Englishman Peter Benenson was sitting on the Tube in London, wearing his bowler hat and looking at a copy of the *Daily Telegraph*. He had just been reading an article about two students in Portugal who had been imprisoned for expressing their beliefs and it struck him that perhaps he should have a go at changing things. That was the beginning of Amnesty International. A year later the organization was up and running, and since then thousands have been helped. In 1975, the Dominican Republic was holding the union leader Julio de Peña Valdéz in custody. After the first 200 letters arrived on the prison's doorstep, he was given his clothes back. After the next 200, the prison's director wanted to meet him. And after 3,000 letters had arrived, the country's president finally gave up and set him free. Today Amnesty is the world's largest independent human rights organization.

It was considered impossible to climb Mount Everest without extra oxygen until the Austrian Peter Habeler and the South Tyrolean Reinhold Messner did so on May 8, 1978. Since they proved that it was possible, Messner has done it solo, and around 200 climbers have followed suit. Messner has also, together with the German Arved Fuchs, skied across the Antarctic via the South Pole. Habeler and Messner's achievement was considered an impossibility until suddenly it wasn't. For any

established but erroneous truth to be disproved, you need someone who can distinguish impossibility from improbability. Keep Amelia Earhart's advice in mind: "Never interrupt someone doing what you said couldn't be done."

6.

Courage Can't Be Kept
in a Thermos

One thing most explorers have in common is this:
When we seek out challenges and dangers, it's not
about playing with death—quite the opposite. We seek
out danger because experiencing intense situations
and having the ability to surmount them feels like a
confirmation of our own existence.

I remember the last metres of Mount Everest.
Just before you come to the absolute summit from
the south-east side, there's a small sub-peak on the
mountain itself. It's called the South Summit. From
this point to the summit proper, the route goes along
a very narrow ridge of ice and snow called the Cornice
Traverse. It's hellishly narrow and incredibly difficult
to climb. To the left as you climb towards the summit,
there's a steep descent of about 2,000 metres into
Nepal. To the right side there's a sheer drop of about

3,000 metres into Tibet. With the exception of the odd small ledge, I reckon that nothing would break your fall before you landed in the bottom of the valley. One of the guys I was climbing with joked that he'd kept a bit to the left when crossing that perilous ridge, the reason being that, if he had fallen, the drop would have been a whole kilometre shorter than if he fell off the right side. I had a good laugh at that, but two days earlier, when—slowly and unsurely—I had climbed along that same treacherous ridge, I had thought only about getting safely to the other side.

Looking down from a great height has always bothered me. I grew no more fond of it climbing Everest, though I was slightly numb because of lack of oxygen. I managed to get over certain elements of my fear in those weeks, but a good proportion of it remained. It was there the whole time. So as not to freak out, I simply didn't look down from the steepest points. The truth is, I didn't dare. Crossing the ridge, I looked forward, meticulously watching the placing of each and every step. I wrote in my journal: "Looking down to the right, and just a little to the left. Making up my mind not to do so again." On those occasions when I did have to look straight down, I simply blocked out all thought of what could happen. I attempted to fix my gaze and my mind on something else with as much bravery as I could. In other words, I had sufficient courage to climb the mountain, but not to look down any more often than was strictly necessary.

Generally speaking, it's not easy to be courageous, nor is it easy to know what courage means. For me, at any rate, both are difficult concepts. Where does courage come from? Fear, a need for recognition, sheer folly, or idealism? When my children jump down from high fences and trees, I think it's a combination of the latter three. Over the years, after giving courage a lot of thought, I've concluded that it isn't a concrete quality. It's not something that one is either born with or not. It's something that develops, something that is fostered or repressed at different times. Courage comes in different forms.

Being brave definitely means having some idea of the consequences of your undertaking. At home many thought we were courageous to set out on an expedition to the North Pole, not least because at times the temperature would drop below minus fifty degrees Celsius. When I travelled around South-East Asia giving lectures, I was met with little response when I quoted such temperatures; it didn't seem like fifty below meant anything at all to my Asian audience. It then occurred to me that they had never experienced the freezing cold and therefore weren't impressed by the idea of someone enduring temperatures like that. By contrast, it was because my listeners had seldom been alone for more than fifty minutes that they were so fascinated by the thought of being alone for fifty days on a solo journey to the Pole.

Courage also doesn't mean carrying on regardless of the consequences, because to be reckless is not to be brave. There's no shame in turning back; that's rule number eight of the Norwegian Mountaineering Code. I've asked myself if one of the reasons why I've seldom turned back may be that I haven't had the courage to do so. It can be a good deal more tempting to expose oneself to extra danger than to be the object of disapproval or mockery. On my first expeditions I reckon that my fear of proving the naysayers right was at times an important motivation for going on. Since then, now that my experience has become more developed, that particular fear has played a less significant role. Yet I happily admit that it is there. The need for recognition has lessened through the years, but that doesn't mean it's vanished. When I climbed Everest, I was so exhausted during the last 300 metres that I fell asleep whenever I sat down on my backpack to take a break. All common sense said that I should turn back. But by that time, I'd stopped listening to reason. All I did was put one leg in front of the other, no matter the cost. I felt like an animal, and I acted out of instinct and nothing more. I've been given credit for my courage that day and for staying the course. Personally, I believe I was neither brave nor cowardly; I was merely dopey and had stopped thinking rationally. Courage presupposes fear, or at least concern for one's safety, and that was something I had neither the wits nor the strength to consider.

The Swedish polar explorer Salomon August
Andrée wanted to be the first to fly to the North Pole
in his hot-air balloon, the *Eagle,* in 1897. The idea was
to let himself be blown northwards from Spitsbergen
by the southern wind. Andrée was totally dependent
on favourable wind and weather conditions. A short
time before his departure, he was informed that the
wind between himself and the Pole was not blowing
in the right direction and that his attempt to fly would
almost certainly fail. With this information at his
disposal, Andrée had to choose between returning
home to abuse and derision or embarking on the
Eagle's journey like a stubborn hero. He didn't have
enough courage to return to Sweden, but he did have
the guts to fly north—despite the strong risk of death.
The corpses of Andrée and his men were not found
until 1930, east of Spitsbergen, on White Island. To
this day Andrée is considered a hero, and Swedish
children are taught of his unrivalled courage. But
for me the expedition's last man, the newly wed Nils
Ekholm, is an even greater hero. This man chose to
withdraw from the expedition when he realized that

in all probability they weren't equipped for the task. He understood that in exposing himself to derision and scorn he was saving his new wife from the agony of grief, financial hardship, and solitude.

A similar story can be found in *The Mystery of Courage* by the American author and professor of jurisprudence William Ian Miller. In 1914, an ordinary soldier by the name of Probert was commanded along with his American battalion to cross the Atlantic to Europe to take up active service. The whole battalion had joined up as volunteers, but Private Probert refused to leave. When the colonel challenged him, Probert replied: "I'm not afraid, Colonel, Sir. But I don't want to be shot at. I have a wife and pigs at home." His fellow soldiers made fun of him, and the colonel did his best to humiliate him too, at first beseeching him to change his mind, and then ordering him to do so. But Probert wouldn't budge. In the end the authorities gave up and he was dismissed from duty. The official reason given was not Probert's lack of willingness to risk his life, but his lack of intelligence. At any rate, the end of the story

was that Probert went home happy and content to
his wife and pigs. Probert was comparable with Nils
Ekholm—he was courageous in his own way. Perhaps
he knew or guessed just how poorly the common
soldier was treated in war, and how awful life was
as a widow. In my eyes he displayed great courage.

When I returned home from Everest, Arne Næss
said it was an impressive feat but that it would have
taken more courage to forget my ego, my single-
minded desire to break a record, and instead to have
turned around five metres below the summit, when
I knew my goal was within reach. I do agree, but by
then it was too late.

It was easier to be courageous when I climbed
Everest and was in the public eye than when I
did things completely unseen. I still would have
climbed Everest if no one had been watching, but it's
undeniable that it's easier to show bravery when we
can be sure of the reward.

I've taken some chances on expeditions. And at
times it's been dangerous, as when I've taken in sail
on a rough sea or sprinted across thin ice. At times

I've been courageous; on other occasions, as I've said, I've barely been aware of what I was doing. Then there are the moments, like when Børge and I were attacked by a starving polar bear close to the North Pole, that we simply did what we had to in order to survive. Having to shoot a charging polar bear close up was a sad setback, but it was a question of who would have whom for dinner. I'm proud of what I've achieved, but when I think of it in terms of courage, I feel I've perhaps been given more praise than I deserve.

Back in Norway I spoke with a woman who worked as a prostitute in our capital. She told me how impressed she was that I had defied cold, wind, and danger to reach my goals. This was on Christmas Eve, and I told her that in my eyes she displayed considerable courage in her daily existence. To trail through Oslo in a miniskirt when it was twenty below, and then jump into a stranger's car—and put herself into the hands of unknown men—that takes guts. We might have had different reasons for doing what we did—experience in my case, survival in hers—but in my eyes we both displayed courage along the way.

Showing courage in day-to-day life is a different challenge altogether. Now and then it strikes me that I'd rather climb Everest again than have to go through what some people face in everyday life, with all its injustice and cruelty. Being responsible for raising three teenage girls seems far more daunting to me than scaling most mountains. It takes so much courage to battle a serious illness, to show kindness, to keep promises, to end relationships—not to mention daring to love and to express love—and to deal with betrayal, disappointments, and sorrow. As the Norwegian psychiatrist Finn Skårderud once asked, "What is a bungee jump compared to waiting for the call of a loved one that never comes?" An expedition lasts for several months; it's hard while it endures, but all those other everyday challenges last a lifetime, give or take a bit. Conducting oneself properly in all of the myriad situations of normal existence, and being honest both with oneself and with others, is often tougher and a greater challenge than a journey where the whole thing will finish at a designated geographic point.

At times it's not easy to know whether greater courage is required to wait than to act. Emily Shackleton, Eva Nansen, and Kathleen Scott were given no choice when their explorer husbands decided to put the ice before them, but they showed unsung courage when home and family had to be held together once the men had set off. When the husbands did not return, the authorities occasionally took care of the hero's family, but most were more or less left to fend for themselves. I reckon that remaining at home with sole responsibility for the family while the father was absent for several years (or perhaps for good) probably demanded greater courage than that which their husbands exhibited.

Although it isn't always easy to know what it is to be courageous, I reckon the majority of us recognize the feeling of courage when we experience it. Like Mufasa in the film *The Lion King,* I think I'm courageous when I have to be. Mufasa sees no point in exposing himself to unnecessary danger; he just lets that pass by. But when his son's life is threatened early in the film, Mufasa risks his life to save him.

The problem with courage is that it isn't something I can simply put in my Thermos and keep warm until the need arises, something that I can just gulp down like a few magic drops to render me brave and courageous. If it was, it would be something akin to the potion that gives strength to Asterix—a case of straightening one's back when the situation demands courage. The fact is that courageous isn't something we are, it's something we become—just as cowardice is not bestowed upon us at birth. Being courageous is a new challenge each and every time the need arises.

7.

Having Something to Lose

Courage presupposes that the challenge has an element of danger. It's great to work hard for a good cause in the office of a charity, but courage is not necessarily demanded. For any undertaking to be truly challenging, you have to stand to lose something. This applies in great things as in small. You might be risking the annoyance or scorn of others, physical danger, or economic uncertainty. When I was a kid, I remember being impressed by a friend, a girl who went against all the fashion trends at school in choosing a highly idiosyncratic dress code all of her own making, even though her parents were more than willing to buy her what she needed. When I think back on it now, I still feel it was quite courageous on her part. Not to mention those who were bullied and who, nevertheless, managed to keep their heads above water and go to school day after day.

When all is said and done, the individual who displays courage must risk something in doing so—a position at work has to be given up, the face of a mountain climbed, a choice needs to be made at the expense of something or someone. If not, what they're doing may be something great, but it's not courageous.

My experience is that on those occasions when I, of my own volition, have risked something in my actions or my speech—chosen the narrow way—life has been given extra meaning. It's always risky to choose your own way, to gamble on what is uncertain. Health, kudos, self-image, money, or life itself may be on the roulette wheel. But not doing it can be dangerous too—and duller. Certainly, the dream of a danger-free and risk-free society is as old as humanity itself and has much to commend it. Politicians in Norway endlessly discuss the possibility of creating it. I'm not saying we shouldn't strive to ensure that as few accidents as possible happen in our day-to-day lives, but life without a little elected risk now and then is not much fun either.

Danger is relative too. The mountaineer Tenzing

Norgay, along with Edmund Hillary, became the first to reach the summit of Everest in 1953. Tenzing Norgay understood the situation so well that as they neared the summit on May 29 at about 11:30 local time, he let Hillary pass him and walk six feet ahead as they reached the goal. To be the very first was of greater importance for a white New Zealander than for a Sherpa, who felt perhaps that his people, in a spiritual sense, had been to the top many times already. But Norgay didn't die with his boots on in an accident on one of his innumerable climbs. He was a keen smoker and died of lung infection. Fridtjof Nansen, who in 1895 set the "farthest north" record, died peacefully at home. It's fitting though, that the last words he wrote in his diary were "farther and farther north." Reinhold Messner managed to climb and descend the fourteen world summits that rise over 8,000 metres, only to be badly hurt after having to climb a wall to an open window of his own house because he'd forgotten his keys. Neil Armstrong died in hospital two weeks after heart surgery. Short stages on the journey can be very dangerous, and

I've often felt civilized life can be just as treacherous as anything I've encountered in the great outdoors, like when I cycle through Oslo to my office, or when children cross the street alone, or when I'm waiting for a taxi late in the evening surrounded by drunk, aggressive people. And if you spend most of your life sitting on your sofa, your chances of heart disease increase.

Our lives will never be free from danger, either above or below the tree line, but when one gambles on one's chosen path, defying danger becomes a desire in itself. Without it, you may as well have gone by helicopter or snowmobile. It's best to minimize danger before and during an expedition, but if it's absent there's no gamble whatsoever. When Roald Amundsen disappeared in the Arctic Ocean, Fridtjof Nansen questioned in his eulogy whether Amundsen—the first through the North-West Passage, the first to the South Pole, and most likely to the North Pole too—had ever known fear worth suppressing. Of course Amundsen did, just like the rest of us. An eternal fear of not succeeding, of the dangers that lay ahead, of not being respected, together with a constant need to break down barriers and take hold of something beyond himself.

I don't want to romanticize danger, but I've always found weighing up the risks puts me in the right frame of mind for the journey. It helps me get an overview beforehand of what could potentially go wrong and how I could contain the situation. Using this process, I am able to determine in advance just how dangerous things are going to be. If I'm paying attention, I'll almost always find safer alternatives. Over time these dangers become part and parcel of daily living; one grows used to them and they become a natural part of one's existence. Without that little bit of uncertainty, I think I'd rather do something else instead.

Optional risk and danger are still, obviously, a luxury. At times, they can be extremely uncomfortable, but we are privileged to be able to afford them, irrespective of whether we are out in the wild or somewhere else. In the old days the vast majority of people in Norway had enough of a battle just keeping body and soul together, for both themselves and their loved ones, and that's still true for many people around the world. I remember my grandfather telling me of the brutal life he endured at the children's home where he grew up from the age of six. His mother couldn't afford to keep him at home after my great-grandfather was washed overboard on the high seas. Daily life thereafter was a struggle for my grandfather: a fight for survival which for the most part meant obtaining food, clothing, somewhere to live, and a smattering of education. I always thought of my grandfather as someone who had a great deal to live for.

Humans need challenges, moments that make us feel like we have to earn the gift of life. Most of our genes are from the Stone Age. When dangers and challenges present themselves, they create meaning, and I feel fundamentally that I'm aware of being alive. Past and future are of no consequence. All that counts is my situation there and then. As for the other stuff—the dream of a lottery win, a better car than the

neighbour's, or any ambitions influenced by others—it no longer has much meaning.

The more my very existence is narrowed down, the stronger and more aware I feel. Urban life is so often about absorbing as many experiences you can in as short a time as possible—it's overkill, which I feel waters down my consciousness. On expeditions it's about the opposite, and I think it's possible to experience something similar almost anywhere. Lewis Hamilton, the Formula One driver, talks about how it feels to be driving into a turn at 190 miles per hour, how the rest of the world is shut out, a calm falls over him, and he observes all the other competitors, the crews, and the curves in slow motion, almost as a fly observes us humans. I experience a bit of the same thing when sailing in storms over the seas or crossing the notorious Khumbu Glacier, next to Everest, but also at home, when I am embraced by someone I love. It feels like time stands still and I'm suddenly not thinking about anything else.

8.

Learning Not to Chase
Happiness

Have you ever asked yourself if you're happy and
wondered why you are? It's something I've done. And
although I felt I was happy when I asked the question,
I began to doubt myself.

One of Aristotle's fundamental ideas is that human
beings who want to live a good life must strive to
develop their potential and to live in accordance
with it. You must not strive for the wrong things,
like wealth or fame. A good life comes from using
one's senses, seeking knowledge, living in fellowship
with others, and being engaged. To put it simply,
contentment will come to one who is content.
Perhaps it's rather dangerous to take just a couple of
ideas from Aristotle's body of work, yet it gives me
great delight to do so because it reminds me that our
fundamental thoughts and challenges remain the

same throughout history, just as much today as 2,300 years ago.

When I've actively searched for happiness, I've never found it. I don't deny that others can find one single absolute meaning for life, but I haven't managed it. In my experience, the meaning of life changes from day to day, from year to year, and from person to person. The challenge for me, therefore, is to find purpose on life's different paths.

Today I live a very different life from the one I did as an adventure seeker. To live dangerously in a physical sense doesn't tempt me as once it did. Family life and exciting work provide me with a purpose I didn't have before in my daily life. Nonetheless, in order to live a fulfilled life, I need to constantly extend my boundaries, set myself tests. That life may be meaningful in all circumstances is something that, for me, is all too easy to forget. It's my choice. It doesn't always need to be something big. A short ski trip, caring for others, reading a good book, showing generosity, being with my children, looking at art, talking to a stranger in the street—all these things can bring just as much joy and meaning as dangling from a rope below the world's highest summit. The latter can even appear meaningless in comparison. As many have noted before me, it's not about finding a single meaning for life but about finding a variety of meanings in life by paying attention moment to moment.

"It is better to be a human being dissatisfied than a pig satisfied; better to be Socrates dissatisfied than a fool satisfied." The first time I read this declaration by the British philosopher John Stuart Mill (1806–1873), I reacted negatively to his rather crass words, but I liked the dilemma and the idea that goals and pleasures are of varying quality. One experience may be qualitatively better than another. There is a big difference between diving into cold water for a refreshing dip and diving into the same water to save a life, although both can give a great sense of happiness. According to Mills, it is better to think for oneself, to make one's choices, and to conduct oneself wisely in relation to the world than not to possess those qualities, even if one considers oneself happier without them. Mill believed that the reason someone can be content with being a happy fool, rather than a discontented Socrates, is that the fool knows only one side of existence, whereas the latter knows both. Because if one knows both sides, one will choose the more authentic, which according to Mill is the choice of greater worth. His conclusion resonates with adventure seekers. When I think of fellow explorers, none of them would have opted for a more comfortable life, even when that means choosing to wake up when it's minus forty degrees Celsius inside the tent.

A great experience few explorers talk about, maybe because it is too obvious to them, is that life in general feels long when you live close to nature and slowly wear yourself out by hiking all day. Many of those I meet in Oslo and other urban areas I've seen in my travels view their lives as short, particularly as they get a little older. I think that is a bit sad. To me they seem to be focusing on their own perceptions rather than acknowledging the laws of physics.

Two thousand years ago the philosopher Seneca wrote with wisdom on how time can be experienced on an emotional level: "You are living as if destined to live forever." He goes on to describe how we humans live through other people and are never centred in our own lives. We are careless with our own time. While we guard our property and social status as if they're the most important things in life, we have a completely casual attitude towards our time, the one thing that we know for a fact to be finite. He who exists "hustles his life along, and is troubled by a longing for the future and weariness of the present." When they come to the end of it, "the poor wretches realize too late that for all this time they have been preoccupied with doing nothing." The nightmare scenario for Seneca is to die while doing your own accounts as your inheritors stand behind you enjoying themselves.

Seneca is, of course, making sweeping generalizations here, but I do agree with him on one point: that our lives will feel long enough if we don't throw our time away. It is about being present in the

moment and living less through other people and
screens.

In September 2002, researchers imaged the brain of
a Buddhist monk—which they measured using a cap
fitted with 256 thin wires—as he gradually worked his
way into deep meditation and the feeling of happiness
which characterizes this state. They could see on the
screen that parts of the brain lit up with electrical
activity as the monk progressed inwards. It made
clear, as American psychiatrist Richard J. Davidson,
who was part of the research team, claimed, that
happiness isn't a vague, indescribable feeling: "It's a
physical state of the brain," something you can induce
deliberately.

   In other words, scientists were in the process of
proving what Buddhists practising meditation have
known for centuries: happiness is a state we can
achieve ourselves that has little to do with what goes
on around us. Parts of the brain are in a constant
state of flux, and we can reprogramme them if we
choose to do so. The research team has, in addition

to plotting the physical characteristics of the feelings of happiness, concluded that what they have seen happen in the brain also affects our legs, our arms, and how we breathe—as most people who have walked or climbed far have felt.

I sometimes try to figure out how happy the people I meet are. In December 2010, the American urban historian and explorer Steve Duncan and I descended into New York's mystical network of sewer, subway, train, and water tunnels to cross from 242nd Street in the Bronx to the Atlantic Ocean, staying underground as much as possible. Walking through Manhattan's Freedom Tunnel on the West Side, we visited a woman named Brooklyn who had lived in the tunnel since 1982. Her home was a concrete space twelve feet above the tracks which she called her "igloo." Her bed was a mattress on the floor, nicely made up. A pile of empty bottles and cans making up the bulk of her possessions was in the corner. A magazine article with photos of Michael Jackson had been torn out and the pages hung side by side on the wall. She also had a photo of herself looking very beautiful.

I was curious about her thoughts on happiness. Steve and I had met Brooklyn on an earlier hike through the tunnel, and we agreed she appeared more happy than most New Yorkers we saw above ground. "How happy are you, on a scale of one to ten?" I asked her. "Seven," she replied, and added, "other times eight." Brooklyn went on to explain that she is the most happy when she has finished searching dumpsters up on the street for food, drink, and clothing and returned to her igloo to feed and play with her cats. And also when she sings hits from the early eighties, around the time when she moved in. As she explained, "It's called 'appreciate what you got.'"

Once, when travelling east to Kamuli in Uganda with my daughters, I got to know a woman who lived with her husband, seven children, and hens in a hut of about forty square feet. There were three beds in the hut but no electricity or water, and there wasn't even a bucket to use as an outhouse. I asked her the same question that I had asked Brooklyn, and she also said seven, but then corrected her answer to closer to eight. Her husband stuck with his answer of seven.

He had two wives and a total of seventeen children. There are two harvest seasons in Kamuli. The couple explained that, close to the harvests, after all their work, a feeling of well-being came to them, especially if it proved to be a good year.

If I ask almost any Norwegian—including myself— to rate their happiness on a scale of one to ten, the answer is usually the same: seven, sometimes eight.

I was made aware of just how little can separate feeling happy from feeling down on the way home from the Caribbean when I was twenty-one. I was in the company of two friends, Hauk Wahl and Arne Saugstad, who were the same age as I, when we hit seriously bad weather in our thirty-five-foot sailboat just north of the Azores. The sails were torn to ribbons by the wind, the hatch in front of the mast was washed overboard, and the boat was on the brink of sinking. In such situations the best pump on the market is frightened kids with buckets, so together we managed to save that boat.

Under such circumstances one's mood changes

more quickly than it normally would. First came desperation when the front hatch was washed overboard and the boat began taking in water; then there was sheer delight when, against all odds, we managed to find the hatch floating in the sea and so were able to rid our vessel of water. Then came pure bewilderment as a monstrous wave literally swept away the mainsail, a situation exacerbated by the fact that we had no engine, the toilet was blocked, and the only cooking appliance was broken. We were living on cold corned beef and potatoes, and damp crackers, and when we had to relieve ourselves, we did it by hanging out from the boat. You can imagine our feeling of joy when we finally reached Brixham, a small fishing town in Devon in south-west England. For the first time since we left the Azores fifteen days earlier, we could walk on solid ground, sit down, and drink without being soaking wet and worried. The point is that all states—both positive and negative— will pass. With the negative ones, you often just have to ride them out.

"Either I'm happy or I'm not, that's all," wrote

the Austrian philosopher Ludwig Wittgenstein. His definition of happiness could well describe that voyage of ours home from the Caribbean. At one moment we felt in heaven, the next in hell.

In *A Wanderer Plays on Muted Strings,* the Norwegian author Knut Hamsun tells the story of a prisoner who's being taken to his place of execution. He is sitting in a cart, and a nail in the seat is snagging his

butt. It's painful, and the prisoner shifts position. At once he feels more at ease. "We all have our softer moments," Hamsun concludes.

Nature has given us pain for our benefit—and pleasure to ensure we're also able to have a feeling of wellness and freedom from a state of pain. The Greek philosopher Socrates was arrested and put in chains. When finally the chains were loosened from his legs and he felt just how sore they had been, he reflected on how wonderful it was to be rid of them. Socrates was keenly aware of the relationship between pleasure and pain, and how those feelings complement each other to our advantage, each eliciting and chasing the other in turn.

I seldom felt a greater sense of well-being than I did on those occasions when, on my way to the North Pole, despite the temperature sinking to fifty below and the food being the same day after day, I could lie down in the tent, feel the warmth flow into my body, and eat to dull my intense hunger. I knew then that Socrates was right. I had no doubt that I was in fine fettle and eating the best cuisine I'd ever tasted. And even today I don't doubt that.

Aristotle thought that a life had to be looked at holistically. If a person succeeds in realizing their potential, then they have had a happy life. The conclusion must wait, in other words, until the end. I have sympathy with this idea, both as an explorer and as a family man. You can only measure a thing like fulfilment by looking at the bigger picture. Short-term happiness seems a little overrated. And I don't think I am always happy when I think I am. It can even be difficult to separate sadness from happiness.

At the same time, I like to stop in my tracks, and just be content with the state of things. For instance, when warmth returns after freezing cold, when a daughter throws her arms around me with joy, when I watch a good football match—then life is good and I feel happy.

9.

Learning to Be Alone

I've felt much more lonely in large gatherings of people and in crowded towns than I did on my way to the South Pole. Far out on the ice, 1,000 kilometres from the rest of humanity, I hardly ever missed the company of others. I missed skin-to-skin contact, but seldom more than that. I had enough: myself, my experience of nature, the rhythm and forward progression of putting one leg in front of the other a sufficient number of times. By contrast, when I was alone in New York for the first time, in the summer of 1986, penniless, knowing no one, my sense of loneliness was oppressive.

Being in a crowd can remind you just how lonely you actually are. On the way to the South Pole I had no contact with the world around me, and perhaps for that reason I missed human contact less. It was a great relief that I couldn't communicate with anyone by radio or phone. To have had such contact would have resulted in some part of my consciousness never having left Norway, and I'd have missed out on a great deal of what the journey had to offer me.

I was reminded of the importance of being at the centre of my own life over the course of that journey. Of not living my life through others. Past and future merged and almost lost their meaning. Nobody could reach me. There was only the present. No TV series, no commercials, no news, no celebrity gossip, no one else to consider. Just enormous white expanses all the way to the horizon. Sun and blue sky twenty-four hours a day (well, almost). A life like that gives one an enormous sense of freedom: the freedom to be alone, and the freedom to follow a dream.

"Loneliness is of course not an asset in and of itself. It often feels like a burden, but it also has potential. Everyone is lonely—some more than others—but no one escapes it," writes the Norwegian philosopher Lars Fr. H. Svendsen in his book *A Philosophy of Loneliness*. Many religions and philosophical systems across the ages have emphasized that loneliness can be something positive, but today many people perceive it as something intrinsically negative. For me it's all about how I respond to the situation of being alone, whether I'm able to harness loneliness in a good way or whether I just become restless or a little frantic. Often I find that I'm restless for the first hours and days that I'm by myself, but usually— if I can stay the course and not allow myself to be tempted into seeking out company or distracting myself by thinking about the past or future—a sense of calm settles over me after a time. Then I can start to enjoy being alone. That experience of loneliness is very close to what is sometimes termed "solitude."

When I was a child, I didn't like being alone. It was generally because no one wanted to play with me, and as a result, I associated it with feeling down. I felt secure when I was around other people—preferably lots of people my own age. I have fine memories of playing ball games with friends in the neighbourhood. In many ways my life as a child was lived through others.

The need for togetherness and recognition from others is part of the human condition. Feeling that you haven't chosen to be alone but that isolation has been imposed on you is very different from electing to spend time by yourself. As a child, I had little notion of enjoying time on my own. On the way to the South Pole, and on other expeditions too, I began to wonder if I had wanted that degree of social contact because I really yearned to be with people, or if it was really because I feared being alone.

The French philosopher and boredom theorist Blaise Pascal wrote about human beings' centrifugal force in the seventeenth century. We are willing to do almost anything it takes to avoid being reminded of our own meaninglessness in the world, and the way to do that most effectively is to be as busy as possible, so we don't have time to stop and reflect. Man, according to Pascal, is the only creature in the universe able to comprehend its own situation. I hadn't read Pascal when I went searching for the South Pole, but his description is very much in line with the realization

I came to on the way: that my motivation for being so social was about running away from myself. And that realization felt crucial.

After I eventually reached the Pole, I was asked if I'd learned much over the course of the journey. To that I emphatically said yes. The journalist then asked what it was I'd learned. To that I didn't have any simple answer. Not because I was in any doubt that those fifty days had been the most educational of my life, but because not all understanding can easily be expressed in words. And for me the journey had begun long before I went to the Antarctic and is still continuing. Today, several years later, I still don't have all the answers to what I learned during those days and nights on the ice. But I do recognize it was during that period of my life that I learned it was possible to live in a different way than I had done before. Being alone, being left to oneself for an indefinite period of time, isn't dangerous. Quite the opposite.

When I came home, my life continued as before. Invoices had to be paid, clothes had to be washed, and when my washing machine broke down, it had to be repaired. The difference was that I was more certain of what was important in my life. I became better at separating things that really meant something from what meant far less, and sorting out which people were of importance to me and which were not. I also knew that now and again I had to be alone, or else I could easily forget just who I was.

I've no intention of going back to Antarctica and spending the rest of my life there. I'm far too fond of family, friends, art, the sea, the woods, and the mountains for that. If you ask almost any philosopher or thinker in history what they think about humans' need for company, the answer will always be this: We are not made to be alone in life. We are mutually dependent on one another.

But it's good to know that I can endure my own company from time to time and to understand that occasional solitary periods do me a lot of good. They enable me to get away from the city, take some time to reflect on challenges in my life, and, by realizing that I miss the company of family and friends, to appreciate

what's important in it. I find that being alone makes me more curious about people—not just those who are close to me but strangers too—to listen to them, to respect them, and to be interested in their troubles and their joys.

10.

Enjoying Small Helpings

Sometimes too much of what's good isn't good; it's simply too much.

"At home I enjoy large helpings. Down here I'm learning to value small pleasures. The subtle shades of the snow. The light wind. Hot drinks. Cloud formations." I wrote this in my journal on the way to the South Pole, on day twenty-two. In the course of three weeks I'd not seen or heard a single sign of life. No people, no animals, no aircraft. I'd put some 500 kilometres behind me and had more than 800 to go. When I began that journey, I felt that everything around me was completely white and flat all the way to the horizon, and that above the horizon it was blue. But over time I'd started to see things differently. The snow and ice were no longer just white but myriad shades of white, and contained glints of yellow, blue, and green. I slowly began to see variations in the flatness—small formations which on closer inspection were like works of art—and different shades of colour worth focusing on.

"It's a clear day. The hugeness of the landscape and the colours of the snow make me happy. Flatness can be beautiful too, not just mountains. I used to think that blue is the colour of poetry, white of purity, red of passion, and green of hope. But here such classifications don't seem natural. Now all of them stand for poetry, purity, love and hope. And tomorrow blue and white might stand for storm and frost."

Your experience of your surroundings can change dramatically over time, even if your surroundings don't change significantly. What alters is what's inside your head. "What in truth is sublime must be sought in the mind of the judging subject, and not in those objects of nature which give rise to the mood," wrote Immanuel Kant. What is beautiful lies in nature, but for our surroundings to be truly sublime, a transformation has to occur between our own two ears rather than in what we see. What appeared as beautiful to me at the outset of my trek to the

South Pole became in the fullness of time a sublime experience. It was all about noticing small details: a mountain on the horizon, the wind, a snow crystal, a formation in the ice.

The stillness in the Antarctic is more profound, and can be heard and felt more clearly, than almost all sounds. Silence is eloquent. At home there's always a radio on, a phone buzzing or vibrating, or a car passing by. There are so many sounds that I barely hear them. In the Antarctic, when there wasn't any wind, the stillness was far more powerful than it was back home. In my journal for day twenty-six I wrote: "Here stillness is all-absorbing. I feel and hear it. In this endless landscape everything seems eternal and without limit. The soundless space does not feel threatening or terrifying, but comforting." At home I barely notice what is happening around me, but there I became so attuned to my environment, so much a part of it, that stillness became part of me, something I could listen to. If I had enough energy for it, I made new discoveries every day. I was completely isolated from anything that lay beyond my horizon, so it was only my nearest surroundings I could relate to. As the weeks passed, my impressions of those surroundings became stronger and stronger. Gradually I worked up a dialogue with them, a dialogue that was dependent on what I could contribute and what I was able to take in. Not a conversation in the normal sense of the word, but an exchange nonetheless where I sent out thoughts and received ideas in return. Towards the end of the journey, on New Year's Eve, I wrote in my journal:

Just as I have felt my own smallness in relation to the natural environment, I've also felt an inner greatness. I've experienced terror and joy, known relief and disappointment, beauty and pain, have asked questions and found some answers, sensed closeness to the elements, given of myself and received, had the joy of physical exertion, and been strengthened in the view that there are still challenges and dreams worth giving one's all for. Although the great truths have not been revealed, I can understand that time in the desert was decisively important for great leaders like Jesus and Buddha. Here one may experience what one cannot elsewhere.

When I think back, it's that closeness to the natural environment which made the greatest impression over those fifty days I was alone in the Antarctic. At times culture and nature can be contradictory, but not on a journey like this. My imagination and my language were good tools for creating a bond with nature rather than distancing me from it. I became a part of the ice, the snow, and the wind over the course of that journey, and that environment gradually became part of me. On the ice and oceans, and in the mountains and forests, I learned that less can be more.

Perhaps thirty was rather late to be coming to this realization. I remember as a child how a small piece of cake tasted better than a big piece, but I never drew any conclusions from that. Each new spoonful tasted less good than the one before, and if I ate enough

I felt sick. That's what economists call the law of diminishing returns. Next time I got the chance to eat cake again, I ate as much as I could stuff down, naturally. But when there was only a small piece to be had, it meant I savoured it.

Now and then I still think it can be good to go whole hog and dig in—but I'm glad I've become aware of the pleasure of enjoying small helpings. Architects, of course, made this discovery long ago. "Less is more" is a principle attributed to the German architect Ludwig Mies van der Rohe. This might be a tad unfair, considering the expression was familiar in architectural circles in Germany before it was officially credited to him. He was, however, one of those who really applied the consequences of this philosophy, and in so doing became one of the groundbreaking powers in modern architecture. He showed that the function and beauty in every object could be highlighted through the omission of certain elements. Its strength as a whole will be increased by using less.

In the Antarctic I had the freedom to choose what I wanted at any time, much as at home. But unlike at home, I was restricted to only a few options from which to choose. When I wasn't on skis, I tried to do at least two things at the same time. To prepare lunch and fill Thermoses while I was reading and eating, and so forth. By and large all these duties were routine and on my to-do list. There was nothing more to choose between or think about. All in all, I was very efficient on the ice, and got done everything I had to do in the course of the day. For example, if it was not too cold, I tried to read a little bit every evening. To save weight, the books I brought had as many thoughts and ideas as possible per gram. Later I recycled the pages I had read as toilet paper.

At home I value having many options and being able to pursue things at will. The more I'm involved, the more I feel I'm getting out of life. From a logical viewpoint, I can't see that that's a bad conclusion. The problem is that at times it can be limiting to have so many tasks to do at once, and so much to choose from. It's lovely to think of being faced with a choice of three different jams at breakfast, but it can also feel excessive and, therefore, wasteful. On expeditions I certainly didn't miss all the alternatives; I simply ate the same thing every day—oats, dried meat, chocolate with extra calories, honey, dried fruit, different sorts of fat, formula milk—and I felt I had earned my meals. The more exhausted I got, the better they tasted.

The secret to a good life, seen from the ice, is to keep your joys simple. That doesn't mean my goal is to live this simply all the time, nor do I believe it's best to be faced with infinite choice. It's about having just enough options to feel like I can choose the one that works for me, but not so many that I feel unable to assess the relative merits of each option. There's not as much difference as it appears between having no options and having a plethora of them. Both situations can render me powerless.

On the eighth day of my journey to the South Pole, I discovered that the oatmeal soup tasted rancid. I was afraid of getting ill and had to throw it away. In my journal I recorded: "I look down on the snow in front of me. The soup has filtered through the snow. The grains of oatmeal and the dried apricots are lying on top. Haven't the heart to let the apricots just lie there. I take off my right glove and pick them up, one by one. It's cold and laborious work. Stuff them into my mouth. Get my glove on. A bit of the sweet taste is left—I relish it." I remember that taste even now, and how those apricots felt in my mouth, and I have no doubt that they're the best I've ever tasted.

I'm not going to tell my children that their lives will be better if they eat a couple of freezing apricots for breakfast. But I hope they won't grow up believing that life is most pleasurable when every meal is a feast. Or that they should sit inside and live in images of the world rather than in the world. If they should ask me how they can balance the great and the small in life, I won't have an inexhaustible supply of answers for them. You will not experience a golden mean for long, your goals may be different the next day, but it's good to strive for balance nevertheless.

One Christmas, when my daughter Solveig was

five, she turned to me after unwrapping her presents and said, "Daddy, I have everything I need in life." I remember thinking that our whole family had something to learn from Solveig that evening. Life feels meaningful when we adopt her outlook.

Now and again I dream about life on the ice, because life out there, in all its simplicity, was uncommonly rich.

11.

Accepting Failure

One of South America's foremost climbers, Rodrigo Jordan, told me that he has made 350 attempts to reach the summit of various mountains. About 120 of these attempts have been successful (of these, three were different routes up Everest). The 230 other times he gave up. "That's why I'm still alive," he concluded.

I was surprised by his relaxed attitude. Of course, I don't doubt that some of the failures had been, and continue to be, both demoralizing and embarrassing, but it's not often I meet someone who understands that success and failure aren't necessarily mutually exclusive. Quite the opposite: one depends on the other, and both are a natural result of risking a little more. If one were never to fail, it would probably be because one didn't gamble sufficiently to start with. The short-sighted view could be that Rodrigo Jordan would have enjoyed many more successes

if he hadn't given up so often, because he'd probably
have summited a good number of the mountains
he hasn't managed to climb. Those with greater
vision, on the other hand, would see that he'd almost
certainly have suffered a serious accident, and in that
sense a really significant failure.

When I was twenty-two, I believed I could make a real
killing on the stock exchange. For a while I managed
to finance my studies this way. Unfortunately for me,
my self-confidence and the stakes rose faster than the
level of my knowledge, and when the market crashed
I lost most of what I had. I hadn't heard of a stop-loss.
The most significant rule I failed to learn was this:
you can't become too invested in your investments.
Otherwise you'll fail to sell them while they're still
valuable. When the market collapsed, I went into a
cold sweat and fretted to such an extent that I was
in physical pain. Today I think back on that time
as a very long day at school, where the curriculum
consisted of learning humility and respect for the
fact that not everything is easily achieved. I've learned

more through failure than success. As Fridtjof Nansen said: "Experience is the best school, but it's exceedingly expensive."

"Pain is temporary. Quitting lasts forever," writes the cyclist Lance Armstrong, in his book *Every Second Counts*. I don't see things that way. Life is by its nature a constant stream of failures, small and large. I don't see mistakes and losses as problems in themselves; it's the way in which I react to them which is decisive. Failure sometimes creates possibilities. And failure is one of the most natural consequences of taking a risk. Perhaps that was the insight Armstrong lacked.

The decathlete Daley Thompson, who I mentioned in chapter 3, was asked what it was like to lose his world record, and to go from being a hero to a has-been overnight. He said something like: "I took it like a real man. I cried for a week." Thompson looked reality in the eye; he was no longer a sports star but a former sports star. He accepted it, was down for a week, then put it behind him. It's important to acknowledge, and by doing so expel, those feelings of grief when the world goes against you, rather than trying to keep a stiff upper lip. And then it's important not to allow those negative feelings to get the upper hand. Bitterness often arises when you don't accept life's realities. It's easy to remain miserable about what was or could have been and to crawl into one's shell indefinitely, instead of searching for new possibilities on the horizon, though it's obviously easier to write about it than to do it.

Being fired or passed over, divorce, financial loss, betrayal, the illness and death of loved ones—these

are setbacks that many of us experience at some point. Such things, of course, can be impossible to recover from. And yet, I think low times also offer new possibilities. It's easy to forget that life is composed of a whole series of single episodes. My ability and will to respond to and absorb what happens to me are critical in deciding whether I weigh up that episode as positive or negative.

I don't know what the composer Beethoven (1770–1827) thought when he lost his hearing, how the painter Goya (1746–1828) coped with the experience of gradually becoming deaf, or how Rembrandt (1606–1669) coped with the death of his first wife or his later bankruptcy when his clients turned their backs on him. I love all three artists. But what I do know is that I consider the Ninth Symphony, which Beethoven composed after he had gone deaf, superior to most, and the paintings Rembrandt produced in the wake of his bankruptcy in 1656 to be superior to his early work—his brush strokes became rougher and the colour incandescent. Had Goya stopped painting in the 1790s, when his hearing began to fail him, we'd never have seen any of the works for which he won such fame.

At times it can seem as though too few failures can weaken artistic development. If a writer's first book wins all sorts of major awards, the second book is often disappointing. A friend who has a gallery in Berlin told me that although he labours just as hard for his first-time exhibitors, trying to sell all their work and make them hugely successful, in his heart of hearts he hopes their first show won't sell out. Some sales are okay, but not too many. "Overnight success doesn't do artistic talent a bit of good," he maintains. Of course, he wishes the artist as a person all the luck in the world, but at the same time he knows their art will suffer if recognition comes too soon or too easily.

Since becoming a publisher, I've observed just

how many mistakes I've made and yet still managed to run a healthy business. In the first years I fretted myself silly over all my failures: good books that we mistakenly turned down, needless expenditures, bad judgement on manuscripts, covers, and the sales potential of different books. One day I met up with another publisher and he told me that mistakes were part and parcel of every publisher's daily existence. It's basically impossible to run a business and not make mistakes. One's goal should be to not make the same mistakes again.

In Britain there's an expression I haven't encountered anywhere else: "heroic failure." There's something stoic about striving that bit extra, in solving problems as each one arises. The manner in which one fails is decisive too; if it's done in the way a Brit considers stylish, an amateurish but heroic attempt characterized by courage and backbreaking toil may be greater than achieving the goal itself. In a land like Norway things are different—either we succeed or we fail. To speak of style in connection with this is outlandish. Have we gone too far in Norway, simply calling failure "failure"? I think so. A failure can be many things. Geir, Børge's and my companion to the North Pole, dislocated a disc in his back when his sled fell off an ice ridge. He had spent two years preparing and ten days in temperatures around minus fifty degrees Celsius, and he was not to blame for the unfortunate accident.

Of all the photos taken on the moon on Sunday, July 20, 1969, the picture of Buzz Aldrin, on the ladder, backing out of Apollo 11 is the one I remember best. He had been training for this moment for years and he was 238,000 miles away from home. It was 170 degrees Celsius below in the shade and 120 degrees in the sun. Aldrin had only one problem in the whole world; Neil Armstrong had already been there for nineteen minutes and was ready to take the picture. Aldrin felt that "silver medal" was a failure. To me, that response demonstrates that everything can be considered defeat. Michael Collins, the third man on board, didn't even step on the moon. He orbited it fourteen times, surrounded by 700 different switches and ten kilos of checklists, while waiting for the other two to do their thing. He was in total darkness behind the moon and in sunlight on the other side. Collins expressed his satisfaction with what he had been permitted to be part of. I think that's wonderful. During the second night he was in quarantine after his return to Earth, he crept back into the capsule and wrote in minute writing:

SPACECRAFT 107—
ALIAS APOLLO 11—
ALIAS "COLUMBIA"
THE BEST SHIP TO COME DOWN THE LINE
GOD BLESS HER
MICHAEL COLLINS, CMP

I still regret failures that I'm to blame for. When I was younger, I think I did so more frequently. More and more people my age have all but stopped doing so now, and have begun instead to regret what they

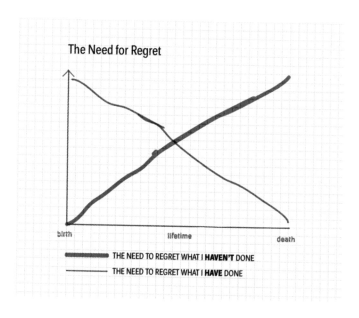

The Need for Regret

birth   lifetime   death

■■■■■■ THE NEED TO REGRET WHAT I **HAVEN'T** DONE

——— THE NEED TO REGRET WHAT I **HAVE** DONE

didn't do. Perhaps it wouldn't have been so silly to have attempted something exciting but risky earlier on in life after all. Perhaps when all is said and done, the mistakes and failures back then were some of our most formative experiences.

12.

Finding Freedom
in Responsibility

When I was a little kid, I dreamed of living free from responsibilities and expectations. I wouldn't have to tidy my room or cut my hair; I'd have enough money and wouldn't go to school. When I was younger still, I even believed that life would be lovely as soon as I was wealthy enough to buy as many sweets as I wanted. Some years ago I saw that my own children, to a greater or lesser degree, were going through a similar phase. They were living in a Barbie economy, where the most significant variable is how many Barbie dolls are available. Life without responsibility seemed the ultimate goal.

There's still a little voice inside that tells me to take the easiest alternative. To go see a film instead of visiting my parents, to put off replying to messages, not to take responsibility for anyone but myself. A make-it-easy-for-myself attitude.

The Austrian psychiatrist Viktor E. Frankl (1905–1997) survived several years in a Nazi concentration camp and said something about his experience which has stayed with me ever since I first heard it: whoever has a why to live for can bear almost any how. We should not wish for less demanding lives, he writes in his book *Man's Search for Meaning,* for life has the potential to be meaningful under all manner of circumstances. Meaning comes from making the best of the situation in which we find ourselves.

Over time, I have realized responsibility is the key to a freer life. If I always choose the path of least resistance, I am not free. If I avoid responsibility, I will always choose the easiest path when I come to any crossroads. In which case, my choices, both great and small, become predestined if I'm looking only for the easiest route. I am shackled by my own desire to be free.

What I once considered a free life (and still occasionally find appealing)—namely, doing as I pleased on each and every occasion, parties, studying, work, skiing, asking girls out at will—doesn't, in other words, appear so free after all. Now it mostly seems an arrogant way to live one's life. In his 2005 commencement address at Kenyon College, the American author David Foster Wallace talked about the importance of paying attention to what's happening right in front of you, rather than becoming preoccupied with abstract ideas. A free life should involve discipline, attention, and awareness, and, of course, generosity. Real freedom is being able "to care about other people and to sacrifice for them, over and over, in myriad petty little unsexy ways, every day." Reading those last seven words always makes me stop and think. The challenge, according to Wallace, is how to find meaning from your experience.

Responsibility and burdens give life substance. If your life doesn't make a difference to others, then in the long run it won't matter all that much to you either. Many people say that being able to choose the right course of action takes wisdom and experience. But I think we know a lot instinctively. It's the choosing

that's the difficult part, no matter how old or wise we become.

As Foster Wallace told the graduating class, taking responsibility isn't always so easy, but "I wish you way more than luck."

13.
Making Flexibility a Habit

At the height of the tech wave at the end of the 1990s, the philosopher Lars Fr. H. Svendsen was asked to produce a report for one of Europe's leading telecommunications companies. His task was to investigate how the company's employees formed habits and how such habits could be broken. The company had just built a new head office and was keen to ensure that none of its employees would bring their old routines into the new workplace.

The problem for Svendsen was that he couldn't see how the firm could manage without routine. The formation of habit is a characteristic of creativity.

Perhaps the company executive had read too much Immanuel Kant. Kant was crystal clear about the fact that it's important to prevent the formation of habit because habit denies us freedom and independence. Kant compares habit to a kind of constraint, in the sense that it becomes similar to a straitjacket from which one can't escape. Or maybe the executive was just following the advice he had read in some business book somewhere. Who knows? But my own experience is that the more tasks I manage to pack into routines, the more time I have left over to do other things and to think.

Kant was also, despite his avowed scepticism on the subject, a very real creature of habit himself, with an enormous capacity for work and creative production. The only thing I still remember about Kant from school is that the citizens of Königsberg—the city, now named Kaliningrad, where he lived all his life—could set their watches by his fixed daily walks.

One of history's least accessible philosophers, Georg W. F. Hegel, who to a considerable degree built his own theories on the works of Kant, described habit as our "second nature"—meaning it was not quite an innate personality trait but one that we turn to, almost automatically. He emphasized that this was something positive which human beings are reliant upon in order to live in a functional way.

When it comes to expeditions, it's my aim to nail as many duties as possible prior to departure, almost in a Hegelian manner. Of course, for me it's more about practicality than philosophy. There are so many decisions to be made in the course of a day in the mountains or on the ice that the fewer questions I have to deal with the better. As I've described before, I had to get up at the same time each day, and my morning routine had to be completed within a specific time. To achieve this, I had to do at least two things at once. For instance, while melting ice to drink I had to carry out any necessary repairs on my equipment. And the very final thing I did each day after breaking camp was to turn and look around to see if I'd forgotten anything. That was vital, because to save weight I had hardly any spare equipment— only a repair kit weighting 1,256 grams—and I will never leave anything foreign in the wilderness. (This is a habit that will not die: every time I leave a table or room, I automatically look around to see if I have forgotten something.) Then I walked for two hours, taking one break of ten minutes—and after nine of

those minutes I got ready to walk again so I wouldn't lose time. I finished every day at a prearranged hour, and having set up camp, I brushed off the snow and moisture from my clothes before crawling into the tent. After eating and some reading, I would lie down to sleep at the very same time each night.

Such rigid structure may seem pedantic and inflexible, but for me it laid the foundation for a good rhythm and inner tranquillity on the journey. When it's stormy, or when forty or fifty degrees of frost are crushing the body, or when that same body is so exhausted it barely obeys orders, then it's vital to have a routine for support. In addition, having certain set patterns of behaviour allows you to enjoy impulsive moments. Habit means that when I'm under pressure, when it's all but impossible to think clearly, I know what to do without thinking, because I've already established what actions to concentrate my energies on. I've found it helpful in my working life too, and when the kids were small and I had to endure endless sleepless nights with them. It's good to know that you're on top of the basics without having to think too much about them, especially when the going gets tough.

Of course, habits can have unfortunate consequences. If followed too slavishly, they can shut out a plethora of opportunities. And they can be taken to a comic extreme. There's a story told about one of the powerful Mexican earthquakes, this one from 1985: a man was found under the ruins of a house but he refused to crawl out. "I can't because I have nothing on," he said. Getting dressed was so ingrained in him that going out without clothes was completely unthinkable.

I've sometimes imagined what would happen if a person became so defined by their habits that their personality ceased to exist. What if they had become such a slave to routine, so predictable, that they could quite simply be swapped with someone else in the workplace, in their circle of friends, and when at home with their partner and children—and no one would be the wiser.

Alternatively, it's easy to imagine an individual who wants to do the opposite of what everyone else does at every given opportunity. To be so impulsive that they are never able to be punctual. The whole time this unusual individual must express just how "out of the ordinary" they are. The irony is that he easily will, despite his best efforts, end up resembling somebody conventional, almost to the extent that he too could be exchanged for someone else without anyone being aware of the swap.

The most exciting artists are almost all bound by routine, at least during those times when they're producing artistic work, though not quite to the extent that they live as I do prior to an expedition, with early mornings and a strict timetable. The stereotypical artist, the wine-swigging or drug-taking artistic soul who has no sense of work routine or adaptability whatsoever, exists too— but isn't as common as we are led to believe. And it's at least my experience that they seldom create great art during such periods of "escape." The Danish-Icelandic artist Olafur Eliasson generally

arrives at his studio every day at the same time—
half past eight in the morning. He does half an
hour of archery to take his mind off everything
else before working solidly for the remainder of
the day. The energy he saves by being systematic
he employs in being creative.

Today, both in my life as a publisher and as the
father of three children, I'm not as concerned with
following set patterns as I am when on an expedition.
Nonetheless, I'm convinced that even in a creative
publishing firm, habit and routine are utterly
necessary. Manuscripts have to be evaluated, worked
on, tidied up, and proofread at least twice after all
the editorial work has been done. There's no point
trying to find a creative way around it. Agreements
and deadlines have to be honoured. Our routines
serve to create time for my colleagues and me to be
impulsive—to make surprising decisions, generate
new ideas for books, and assess new opportunities.
By doing so I achieve more joy for my colleagues as

well as joy for myself as an employer and shareholder. This way, I hope the workplace is more fun than it might otherwise be.

And one aspect of habit that often gives me delight, and which people who constantly need to be spontaneous or unusual cannot enjoy, is that lovely feeling every now and then of simply not giving a damn about a habit when the moment feels right.

14.

Being Proactive with Luck

"Victory awaits he who has everything in order—it's called good luck. Defeat is certain for he who has neglected to take the necessary precautions in time—it's called bad luck."

These words come from Roald Amundsen's account of how he became the first in history to reach the South Pole. Bold words, but accurate nonetheless. Amundsen trusted his fifty-two Greenland dogs and his men, while his competitors had less confidence and experience, and were hedging their bets with horses, motorized vehicles, dogs, and man hauling. Amundsen had another big advantage: he had spent time with the Inuits as he sailed through the North-West Passage some years before and had learned about hunting, food, anoraks, footwear, gloves, and sledding under extreme conditions. This was a time when people in Europe and the United States were sure that we had nothing to learn from indigenous peoples and looked down on their experiences and knowledge.

How the day will turn out can be well and truly decided even before one leaves the tent in the morning. And probably before the expedition has even begun.

"If you make it, people will think you were lucky with the weather" was the last thing the Norwegian artist Jakob Weidemann, our main sponsor for the expedition to the North Pole, said to Geir, Børge, and me before we left. I didn't think about his remark until after we'd come back from the Pole and one person after another asked if we'd been lucky with the weather. Weidemann was a wise man.

Being lucky isn't about being more intelligent than other people or having special physical prowess. On the contrary, luck is about how we behave, what we think and feel. Of course, it's possible to have pure luck, to the extent that one attains something almost as a result of chance. Ringo Starr was a cool guy and a good drummer in the right place at the right time, for example. There's the story of a lottery winner who'd chosen the number forty-eight because for seven nights in a row he'd dreamed of the number seven, and seven times seven is forty-eight, right? Well, no, actually, but that's the number he gambled on.

But there's a big difference between the kind of luck one has once in a while and more systematic luck. It's the latter I'm interested in, because it is definitely possible to argue that Roald Amundsen and countless others like him were blessed with something resembling systematic good luck, in the same way you could argue that great sailors have had luck with the wind. If we consider some of the global successes—photography, insulin, penicillin, the artificial production of nitrogen, and the contraceptive pill—they're all seemingly the result of chance.

Ideally I should be prepared for every eventuality, but it's difficult to imagine that being possible. You can plan yourself to death. Conditions change, and my ability to respond to them is dependent on the time available to me along the way. Unforeseen and awkward circumstances will always arise, but the aim must be to limit them. If I'm successful in this respect, chances are I'll have enough energy and resources to solve the challenges I haven't bargained for when they arise.

Simply deciding what to wear on my feet is a major task prior to setting out on each expedition. "Keep your feet warm and your head cool," as a Norwegian saying goes. Amundsen called it "the great goal" to come up with the perfect footwear solution. He spent two years designing and trying out boots before his expedition to the South Pole.

When I finally set off on an expedition, there's a certain satisfaction in knowing I've done everything I could have beforehand. And more often than not, I feel like I'm attracting good fortune when I've done my homework. Possibilities pursue me. At other times I've been badly prepared. On those occasions it feels like I'm constantly on the defensive. Before I've solved one problem, another has arisen. Then it feels as if bad luck is stalking me.

Before every expedition I've been on I have spent night after night sweating about my preparations.

And although I probably worry more than is necessary, it's definitely better than the alternative. "Be wary then; best safety lies in fear," says *Hamlet*'s Laertes to his sister, Ophelia, as they are about to part. I think that's good advice to give someone you love.

If I grow too sure of myself, I become rather arrogant and not sufficiently self-critical. Then it's easy to overlook the small (or sometimes not-so-small) things that I should have noticed. All in all, it's important to be a bit anxious, not only when making preparations but until such time as the goal is reached. My experience is that most accidents happen when descending mountains, when you feel happy and confident after having summited.

Preparations are all about foreseeing difficulties. The rock climber Alex Honnold tries to visualize all possibilities before he climbs because he does not want to climb halfway up and suddenly be surprised. If I start fretting over every eventuality, knowing I can't do anything to prevent them, then the chances are I'll start making excuses not to set off in the first place.

For me, positive thinking is part of preparation. I have a small but decisive bit of lore I actually think is completely self-taught; I've simply made up my mind not to think negatively about something once I've begun: "This is something I'm going for. With heart and head, until it's proved undoable." This applies as much to big things as to small. There are plenty of good reasons for cursing on an expedition, but doing so can all too easily encourage a negative frame of mind.

Sometimes I think we spend too little time preparing for the important decisions in life, and yet we waste time in sweating the small ones. I am surprised at the way otherwise level-headed individuals will make an offer on a house after being whisked once around the property. Buying a home is, for most of us, the biggest investment we'll make in life, but I have the impression that few do anything but rely on that first impression.

Over the years many people have sought guidance on starting up a business, and still more have asked me for advice on planned expeditions. From the

questions they ask I'm able to get a sense, fairly swiftly, of whether they'll have bad luck with the weather—or not—on the way. Much will be determined before they even set off. Of course, bad luck can befall anyone. You're hit with week after week of storms. There's a media strike the day you e-launch an important book. An apparently trustworthy individual breaks your trust and leaves you in the lurch. But my point is that difficult situations are always going to arise. The question is what you do before they hit. And how you react when they do.

15.

Allowing Goals to Come to Me

I quite often hear that the way to achieve your goals
is to imagine in great detail all the different ways that
success will affect your life. To write down exactly
why you're aiming for something. Perhaps in some
instances that works, but I am inclined to think that's
not always the best way. I certainly don't believe it's
that simple when it comes to polar exploration. It is
absurd to climb Everest, just as it is absurd to walk
to the poles, and that makes it pretty difficult to fully
explain the drive in a rational way. As philosopher and
mountaineer Arne Næss replied when a journalist
asked why he had started climbing: "Why did you stop?"

The fact is that there's very rarely one single reason
for what we do. Some of our motives are very clear
before we start out on an expedition—curiosity, love
of nature, recognition, and the fact that we were born
to explore. These are the things that spur us to action.

But while some motives aren't that easy to identify or may be different according to each person's circumstances, I believe, from my own experience and from my encounters with others, that there are some motives which are behind almost every expedition. Out in the wide world, momentary flashes of experience can be compared to eternity. A few tenths of a second can feel like forever. Past and future are meaningless when I cross a dangerous fissure in the ice. The split second and eternity need not be contradictory. Time is banished, and both things can be experienced at one and the same moment.

Such an experience may be a good reason to walk rather than drive, or to sail rather than fly over the ocean. It's enriching to decide to arrive somewhere under my own steam and experience the journey over time, rather than just running to the fixed point.

"Why walk alone to the South Pole instead of going by helicopter?" is a question I have been asked many times. For me it's always been a given that the former is more rewarding than the latter. The cold, the wind, and all those steps are themselves a purpose.

I often think our real goals—the ones that guide and shape our lives—aren't those that we actively pursue with pen, paper, and a detailed five-year plan in hand. In my experience, our real goals are the ones that are constantly there in the background. They might not be fully formed yet, and they might not make perfect sense, but we just can't seem to shake them. Those are the goals that seem to pursue us and they are the ones that have the most potential to change the course of our lives.

I spent the first decades of my life chasing different goals. When I was a kid, I wanted to be like other kids. That was a goal in itself. I'd be as good at arguing as one, as rich as another, as good a footballer as a third, as handsome as a fourth, and as likeable as a fifth. Five fine goals, but after a time I saw that I wasn't going to reach any of them. And that others wouldn't either, for that matter. It's one thing to have ideals, but it's another to dream of being like someone else. We humans are too different: simultaneously, both you

and the person you seek to emulate are changing—
constantly. It's too easy to run away from oneself.
I was chasing goals that weren't really mine, and
therefore I was never going to achieve them.

In my twenties I slowly started to see that my goals
would eat me alive. I changed my focus and started
to think about my background dreams, the ones that
I had turned away from but which had never gone
away. Becoming an explorer felt like I was following
a predestined path.

As a child, Roald Amundsen slept with his
window wide open through the bitter winter,
preparing to be the first in history to walk to the
North Pole. Then, in 1909, the American explorer
Frederick Cook returned from the Arctic and
claimed to have reached the Pole in 1908. Soon
after Cook's return, another explorer from the
United States, Robert Peary, claimed it was he
and not Cook who was the first. Amundsen was
bitterly disappointed to have been beaten to his

dream. But not for long. Soon the idea of walking to the South Pole came to him. He was already well prepared for the polar regions, after all. He quite literally did a 180-degree turn. When, on December 14, 1911, he stood at the South Pole, he remarked drily: "Never has any man stood so diametrically opposed from his desired destination."

Mullah Nasruddin, the thirteenth-century satirist who brought humour and wisdom to Sufi culture, tells a different tale. Once, a man found him searching for something on the ground outside his house. When asked, Nasruddin replied that he was looking for his key. The man joined him in the search, but in due course asked the mullah: "Where exactly did you drop this key?"

The mullah answered happily: "Inside my house."

"Then why on earth are you looking here?" the man asked, quite baffled.

"Because there is more light here than there is in my house," replied the mullah.

Nasruddin is searching for the key in the wrong place—a bit like those who would love to be bestselling writers but ignore the fact that they actually have to write a whole book first.

In his foreword to the seventy-third edition of *Man's Search for Meaning*, Viktor E. Frankl described how he wrote the book in nine consecutive days. To his surprise, the book became an instant bestseller. Perhaps it did so precisely because commercial

success wasn't his aim. He focused on writing a good and important work by his own standards, not simply one that would appeal to others. As he himself stated: "Success, like happiness, cannot be pursued." The more you aim for success, the more likely you are to miss it. To Frankl, success was merely a side effect of his personal dedication to a greater cause, and it pursued him because he "had forgotten to think of it."

Of course, there's no magic spell for achieving your goals, life-defining or otherwise. I don't always achieve mine. But I find it invariably helpful to reflect on past ambitions. Both the ones I didn't satisfy— when I was rejected by the girl I was keen on, almost sank in the Atlantic, failed as a speculator on the stock exchange, tried to earn money in the blink of an eye without first learning what such a feat required— and the ones I did. In theory, the recipe is pretty simple. On those occasions when I've taken a longer but richer route, the goal or goals have often come closer, almost of their own accord.

16.

Resetting the Compass

In 1985, Garry Kasparov won the best of twenty-four games against Anatoly Karpov to become the youngest chess champion ever. One of the first people he spoke to after his victory was Rona Petrosian, widow of the former world champion Tigran Petrosian.

"I'm sorry for you," she said. "Because the best day of your life is over."

Kasparov had—thanks to his talent, his purposeful training, and an overprotective mother who kept him away from other temptations—achieved what had been his absolute goal in life, at the tender age of twenty-two. He expected to be overwhelmingly happy, but pretty quickly he was simply bewildered. Now what? What Kasparov basically needed was a new dream. He calls it "champion's dilemma."

Magnus Carlsen became the world chess champion

in 2013. Shortly before he won the title, my company published a book about his career. During the writing of it I asked him how he would be able to stay motivated as more and more of his dreams were fulfilled. Carlsen didn't have a good answer. In March 2019, after several world championships, I asked him the same question. This time he had an answer: "My motivation is to learn. I feel there are still so many things in chess that I don't know." Interestingly, he is wondering whether all the new knowledge will be an advantage: "I don't know whether that will lead to playing better." I get the impression that he finds it almost strange to think about how little he understood of the game six years earlier, when he became world champion for the first time. Chess is a sophisticated game: after three opening moves, there are nine million possible positions. But each and every life holds far more possibilities than a chessboard.

The problem for many of my colleagues within the expedition world is that their ambition rests on the fulfilment of a single goal: of scaling a certain mountain or of reaching one particular place. In that way they are a bit like Garry Kasparov, who thought only of becoming world champion, and they risk suffering from the same sense of loss that he did once they achieve it. I don't know just how many times I've heard of that emptiness experienced by adventure seekers once their goal has been reached. The excitement leading up to the moment they succeed and then the downward spiral once there is nothing left to strive towards. And I've experienced it myself. I remember what it was like to reach the South Pole and feel that I was standing at the end of the rainbow. I nearly forgot my other dreams.

It became vital for me to reach new goals. The Norwegian philosopher Peter Wessel Zapffe wrote about something that could be called an explorer's dilemma. The life of an explorer has to end tragically: after the explorer has achieved something extraordinary, the public expects more, and the explorer is, at some point, either not able or unwilling to try. Soon after, they are forgotten, as was Roald Amundsen after his great expeditions. Or the explorer tries to do something even more challenging than last time and fails, or starts to cheat, like Lance Armstrong, to make their accomplishments more impressive.

Mount Everest, the third pole, was my goal—to be the first to reach the world's three poles. I'm not saying that these expeditions were all about achievement for me. I believe that experiences of the natural world should be exactly that, and not about making or breaking records. On the other hand, I don't doubt that personal achievement is a big motivator for most explorers, though they often fail to mention it when they go on about peace, conservation, climate, and cultural harmony. It's fairly clear to me, at any rate, that if I'd been concerned first and foremost with the view, one of the neighbouring peaks would have sufficed: much cheaper, less tiring, and a better vista. In addition to everything else, I would then have seen the world's highest mountain up close.

Once I'd climbed Everest, I knew in my heart I had to keep thinking more expansively. I was on the point of completing all the adventures I had dreamed of. What happened, almost of its own accord, was that all of a sudden I became a father for a first, a second, and then a third time. It was a wonderful surprise. A dream fulfilled, and this in turn gave birth to innumerable new dreams and visions. Tongue in cheek, I've called my role as father "the fourth pole." It was certainly the easiest to reach, but by far the most demanding thereafter.

In the winter of 2005, I was in Copenhagen with a friend. One morning we walked across City Hall Square. It was bitterly cold, and as usual at that hour there were some homeless folk standing huddled just beyond the railway station. One of these fellows came over to sell a newspaper that benefits the homeless, for which 50 per cent of the money goes to the person selling it. We all had plenty of time, so we stood there talking. He was freezing cold and felt bitter towards a society he believed had failed him—but he still managed to be good-humoured. Once again it struck me how alike we all are—born in the same corner of the world, curious, similar language and humour, same age—even though we live such apparently different lives.

So I bought a copy of the paper this guy was selling. On the front page there was an article about dreams, about how difficult it can be to put them into words, and how vital it is to try nonetheless. The article described a survey in which many homeless addicts had been asked what dreams they had. Most said that they had no dreams whatsoever. I could see why someone in their position would feel like this. I have trouble defining my own dreams at times. But it was the last line of the article that has stayed with me ever since: "Oh yes you do have dreams. Please dream again."

As an explorer I often think that nobody knows anything for sure. I don't know which peaks will suddenly appear before me that I'll choose to climb, and which I'll decide to leave alone. I do think that having dreams, and wondering about the world around me, is what will keep me going, whichever route I take. And I'll try to stick to my own philosophy where I can, even though I slip up now and then, and will probably continue to do so. Of all the rules I've set for myself over the years, there are two that I consistently try to stand by.

First: Be kind. Every day. Even on a solo expedition you are depending on dozens of others—the ones who make your boots, tent, sleeping bag, and anorak; the nutritionist; the sponsors—and kindness is met by helpfulness. To be nice is one of the most sensible things to be, and when your life may depend on those people, it is even utterly stupid not to treat everybody well.

The second is an unwritten rule of the mountains and forests in Norway: namely, that you should always leave the site of your camp as it was before you came, or in better shape. I think that is the best rule we have in Norway. The only thing you should leave behind is a sense of gratitude. Gratitude for having had a break and for being on the move once again. The best things in life have no lasting forms. When you move on, don't think too much. Look around you and up, into the sky—towards the sun, the moon, the stars—and listen to the surroundings: the rain falling, your foot rising from the wet moss, and the silence. Ask yourself: Where am I right now?

Thanks. I am here.

Notes

Foreword: Grounding Myself in Nature

Giles Whittell, *Snow: The Biography* (London: Short Books, 2018).

3. Training Myself in Optimism

Martin Seligman, *Learned Optimism: How to Change Your Mind and Your Life* (New York: Alfred A. Knopf, 1990); I can no longer remember where and when I heard the Zen stories; the quote by Paul Vivek appeared in *Fortune*, Europe Edition, March 21, 2005.

5. Not Mistaking Probability for Possibility

Pierre Berton, *The Arctic Grail: The Quest for the North West Passage and the North Pole, 1818–1909* (New York: Viking, 1988); https://en.wikipedia.org /wiki/Polaris_expedition; *Dogtown and Z-Boys* (dir. Stacy Peralta, Sony Pictures Classics, 2001, film); Arne Næss, *Hvor kommer virkeligheten fra? 18 samtaler med Arne Næss* (Oslo: Kagge Forlag, 2000); the information on Peter Benenson has been taken from his obituary in *The Economist*, March 3, 2005.

6. Courage Can't Be Kept in a Thermos

William Ian Miller, *The Mystery of Courage* (London: Harvard University Press, 2000).

7. Having Something to Lose

Tenzing Norgay, "The Great Mystery," in *Everest*, ed. Peter Gillman (London: Little, Brown, 2001); Fridtjof Nansen, *Eventyrlyst*, ed. Erling Kagge (1942; Oslo: Kagge Forlag, 2011); Charles Taylor, *Sources of the Self: The Making of the Modern Identity* (Cambridge: Cambridge University Press, 1989); Scott Shane and Sarah Kliff, "Neil Armstrong's Death, and a Stormy, Secret $6 Million Settlement," *New York Times*, July 23, 2019.

I talked to Lewis Hamilton about how it feels to be driving into a turn at 190 miles per hour in Sicily in the summer of 2018.

8. Learning Not to Chase Happiness

The stories about Brooklyn and the family in Kamuli, Uganda, were originally published in my book *Under Manhattan* (World Editions, 2015).

Seneca, *On the Shortness of Life*, trans. C. D. N. Costa (New York: Penguin Books, 2005); Aristotle, *The Nicomachean Ethics*, ed. Hugh Tredennick, trans. J. A. K. Thomson (London: Penguin Books, 2004); Paul Guyer, ed., *The Cambridge Companion to Kant* (Cambridge: Cambridge University Press, 1992); Knut Hamsun, *En vandrer spiller med sordin* (1909; Oslo: Gyldendal, 1993); *Science*, December 3, 2004.

"Either I'm happy or I'm not, that's all" was taken from a diary entry made on July 8, 1916, cited in Wittgenstein's *Nachlass* manuscript, no. 103, p. 18r. The text was posthumously published in Ludwig Wittgenstein, *Notebooks/Tagebücher 1914–1916,* ed. G. H. von Wright and G. E. M. Anscombe (Suhrkamp, 1960; Blackwell, 1961). The story about Socrates and the relevance of pain I read in Michel de Montaigne, *The Complete Essays,* ed. and trans. M. A. Screech (London: Penguin Books, 1993). The essay is called "On Experience."

Peter Travers, "Alex Honnold Documentary 'Free Solo' Is as Extreme as the Man," *Rolling Stone*, September 27, 2018; Daniel Goleman and Richard Davidson, "How Meditation Changes Your Brain—and Your Life," *Lion's Roar*, May 7, 2018.

9. Learning to Be Alone

Aristotle, *The Nicomachean Ethics,* ed. Hugh Tredennick, trans. J. A. K. Thomson (London: Penguin Books, 2004); Lars Svendsen, *A Philosophy of Loneliness* (London: Reaktion Books, 2017).

10. Enjoying Small Helpings

Immanuel Kant, "Of that estimation of the magnitude of natural things which is requisite for the Idea of the Sublime," *The Critique of Judgement,* chapter 26, tr. James Creed Meredith (Whitefish, MT: Kessinger Publishing, 2004).

11. Accepting Failure

Lance Armstrong and Sally Jenkins, *Every Second Counts* (New York: Broadway Books, 2004); Nick Baylis, "On the Science of Happiness," *The Times* (London), December 18, 2004; Will Carling and Robert Heller, *The Way to Win: Strategies for Success in Business and Sport* (London: Little, Brown, 1995). The book has some amusing asides on Daley Thompson.

12. Finding Freedom in Responsibility

Viktor E. Frankl, *Man's Search for Meaning* (London: Simon & Schuster, 1997). Frankl is furthering Friedrich Nietzsche and his well-known quote: "He who has a why to live for can bear almost any how."

"David Foster Wallace, in His Own Words," *Economist,* September 19, 2008, https://www.1843magazine.com/story/david-foster-wallace-in-his-own -words.

13. Making Flexibility a Habit

Paul Guyer, ed., *The Cambridge Companion to Kant* (Cambridge: Cambridge University Press, 1992).

I talked to Lars Svendsen about his experiences in the spring of 2004; I visited Olafur Eliasson in his studio in Berlin in 2004.

14. Being Proactive with Luck

Roald Amundsen, *SYDPOLEN. Den Norske sydpolsferd med Fram 1910–1912* (1912; Oslo: Kagge Forlag, 2004); William Shakespeare, *Hamlet,* ed. Harold Jenkins (London: Routledge, Arden Edition of the Works of William Shakespeare, 1993).

The story of the lottery winner was made up by Professor William Ziemba and cited by Tim Harford in "Resolving Readers' Dilemmas with the Tools of Adam Smith," *Financial Times.*

Mary Wakefield, "If I Get an Adrenaline Rush, Something's Gone Wrong: An Interview with *Free Solo*'s Alex Honnold," *Spectator USA*, February 7, 2019.

15. Allowing Goals to Come to Me

Viktor E. Frankl, *Man's Search for Meaning* (London: Simon & Schuster, 1997); books on Mulla Nasruddin by Idries Shah and various websites on Nasruddin; Christophe Mory, *Ernst Beyeler: A Passion for Art: Interviews*, trans. Isabel Feder (Zurich: Scheidegger and Spiess, revised edition, 2011).

16. Resetting the Compass

Diane Coutu, "Strategic Intensity: A Conversation with World Chess Champion Garry Kasparov," *Harvard Business Review*, April 1, 2005; Peter Wessel Zapffe, *Kvalificerede katastrofer bestemmelse av det objektivt tragiske, Om det tragiske* (1941; Oslo: Pax Forlag, 1996).

To always leave the site of your camp as it was before you rested and to feel gratitude is not only a Norwegian idea. According to French author Sylvain Tesson, in his book *The Consolations of the Forest,* translated by Linda Coverdale (New York: Rizzoli Ex Libris, 2013), Robert Baden-Powell's similar advice was "When through with a campsite, take care to leave two things behind. Firstly: nothing. Secondly: your thanks." I have searched for but not found this quote in other places. Tesson suggests it should be made a universal principle. A very good idea.

My own books have also been used as source material in several of the chapters.

Nordpolen: Det Siste Kappløpet (Oslo: Cappelens, 1990).
Alone to the South Pole, trans. Susan Schwartz (Oslo: Cappelens, 1993).
Under Manhattan, trans. Becky L. Crook (London: World Editions, 2015).
Silence: In the Age of Noise, trans. Becky L. Crook (New York: Pantheon Books, 2017).
Walking: One Step at a Time, trans. Becky L. Crook (New York: Pantheon Books, 2019).

Acknowledgements

Thanks to my American publisher, the late Sonny Mehta; my editor, Edward Kastenmeier; and Caitlin Landuyt. Thanks also to my Norwegian editor, Joakim Botten, and to Rosanna Forte, Petter Skavlan, Gabi Gleichmann, Nick Baylis, Kristin Brandtsegg Johansen, Lars Fr. H. Svendsen, Morten A. Strøksnes, Knut Olav Åmås, Astrid de Vibe, Lars Lenth, Guro Solberg, Yonca Dervisoglu, and the late Arne Næss for commenting so generously on the text; all twenty-five colleagues at Kagge Forlag; Hans Petter Bakketeig at Stilton Literary Agency and Annabel Merullo at Peters, Fraser and Dunlop; and my family.

Thanks also to my friends from my many expeditions— crossing the Atlantic Ocean in *Jeanette IV* in 1983 and 1984: Hauk Wahl, Morten Stødle (Morten was injured, so he couldn't make the return voyage), and Arne Saugstad; going to the North Pole in 1990: Geir Randby (Geir suffered a slipped disc after ten days and had to give up) and Børge Ousland; climbing Everest in 1994: Ang Dorje, Nima Gombu, Norbu, David Keaton, Hall Wendel, David Taylor, Ekke Gundelach, Hellmut Seitzl, Kami Tenzing Sherpa (Kami helped me a lot before the journey), Ed Viesturs, and the inimitable Rob Hall, who passed away peacefully just below the summit of Everest in May 1996; crossing Vatnajökull in Iceland in 2010: Haraldur Örn Ólafsson and Børge Ousland; and walking in New York City: Steve Duncan plus friends who joined us for parts of our journey.

Image Acknowledgements

Many of the photographs in this book are my own, taken on the expeditions I discuss in its pages. I am otherwise very grateful to fellow adventurers for allowing me to use their photographs: Børge Ousland for the images on pages viii–ix, xi, 34, 56–57, 118–19, 124–25, 131, 138–39, 149, 160–61; Kjell Ove Storvik for the images on pages x–xi, 20–21, 67, 90, 98–99, 146, 158–59; the late Rob Hall for the image on page 61; David Keaton for the images on pages 41 and 147; Haraldur Örn Ólafsson for the image on page xvii; and Lars Ebbesen for the illustrations on pages 17 and 114. I would also like to thank the Grenna Museum for the images of Salomon August Andrée's expedition on pages 48–49 and 51; NASA Image Collection/Alamy Stock Photo for the image of the *Kon-Tiki* raft on page 7; Ceal Floyer and Esther Schipper for the reproduction of Ceal Floyer's *Snow Globe* (2017, edition 11/30), photo © Andrea Rossetti on page v.